MAKING OF THE
MODERN FRENCH MIND

HANS KOHN

Professor of History
The City College of New York

AN ANVIL ORIGINAL

under the general editorship of

LOUIS L. SNYDER

D. VAN NOSTRAND COMPANY, INC.

PRINCETON, NEW JERSEY

TORONTO   LONDON

NEW YORK

To

WALLACE SOKOLSKY

D. VAN NOSTRAND COMPANY, INC.
120 Alexander St., Princeton, New Jersey (*Principal office*); 24 West 40 St., New York, N.Y.
D. VAN NOSTRAND COMPANY (Canada), LTD.
25 Hollinger Rd., Toronto 16, Canada
D. VAN NOSTRAND COMPANY, LTD.
358, Kensington High Street, London, W.14, England

Library of Congress Catalog Card No. 55-6243

PRINTED IN THE UNITED STATES OF AMERICA

PREFACE

Modern France was born in 1789. Since then she has been the pioneer and the laboratory for the development and test of liberal democracy on the European continent. Yet democracy never knew there the secure and unbroken growth that characterized the political and social life of the last two centuries in Great Britain and the United States. The French Revolution, with its declaration of human rights limiting the power of government, was never accepted by the entire French people. Conflicting trends and traditions have, for the last 165 years, struggled to shape the modern French mind.

Nineteenth-century France was the center of all the intellectual and social controversies that determined in the nineteenth and twentieth centuries the history not only of France but of continental Europe. Nowhere were the characteristic ideas of the age expressed with similar clarity and insight. Today, as so often since 1789, France finds herself again at the crossroads between a stable, liberal democracy and authoritarian creeds from the Left and the Right. The Western world wonders anxiously in which direction France will go; for her decisions may again influence the fate of continental Europe. A study of the forces which entered into the making of the modern French mind will help us to understand France's ever-threatened and yet victoriously reemerging liberal democracy and to appreciate her rôle in Europe and in the nascent unity of the free Western nations.

I am indebted to my friend and colleague, Louis L. Snyder, for his encouragement and initiative to which this book is due, and to Miss Gertrude Richman, Miss Ruth Sender, and Miss Barbara Benjamin for their intelligent help in preparing the manuscript for the press.

HANS KOHN

TABLE OF CONTENTS

Part 1

MAKING OF
THE MODERN FRENCH MIND

FRANCE'S EUROPEAN LEADERSHIP

France in Her Zenith. In 1685 France held a position of leadership in the Western world as no other power ever did. The great English historian, Thomas B. Macaulay (1800-1859), brilliantly described France's sun at its meridian: "France united at that time almost every species of ascendancy. Her military glory was at the height. She had vanquished mighty coalitions. She had dictated treaties. She had subjugated great cities and provinces. She had forced the Castilian pride to yield her the precedence. She had summoned Italian princes to prostrate themselves at her footstool. Her authority was supreme in all matters of good breeding, from a duel to a minuet. In literature she gave law to the world. The fame of her great writers filled Europe. No other country could produce a tragic poet equal to Racine, a comic poet equal to Molière, a trifler so agreeable as La Fontaine, a rhetorician so skillful as Bossuet. The literary glory of Italy and Spain had set, that of Germany had not yet dawned. The genius, therefore, of the eminent men who adorned Paris shone forth with a splendor which was set off to full advantage by contrast. France, indeed, had at that time an empire over mankind, such as even the Roman republic never attained. For, when Rome was politically dominant, she was in arts and letters the humble pupil of Greece. France had, over the surrounding countries, at the same time the ascendancy which Rome had over Greece, and the ascendancy which Greece had over Rome. French was fast becoming the universal language, the language of fashionable society, the language of diplomacy. At several courts princes and nobles spoke it more accurately and politely than their mother tongue."

France's unique grandeur in the seventeenth century was even more remarkable by contrast with her weakness in the preceding age. The many wars between the house of France and the house of Habsburg in the first half of the sixteenth century were followed in its latter half by the unending civil wars between the Catholics and the Huguenots. The Edict of Nantes in 1598 finally brought religious peace. It established no freedom of church; it introduced merely a limited tolerance. Yet it gave to Cardinal Richelieu (1585-1642) the opportunity to lay the firm foundations of absolute monarchy in France, a monarchy which became under Louis XIV the model for all continental courts.

France's Decline. A slow decline began to set in with the revocation of the Edict of Nantes in 1685. The step was intended to strengthen the unity and uniformity of the absolute monarchy and the official Faith: *un Roi, une foi, une loi*. In reality this abolition of limited tolerance weakened the French state and also the hold of the Catholic church upon the French mind. French political leadership was eclipsed by Britain which was advancing rapidly in the new climate of freedom of opinion introduced by the Glorious Revolution. Britain's political institutions and her experimental science—both opposed to the absolutist concepts dominant in France—became the foundations of her new power. In the eighteenth century Britain took over most of France's imperial position in North America and Asia and successfully disputed French hegemony over the continent of Europe. The contrast between Britain's rising power and France's political and economic decline revealed the insufficiency of the absolutist régime in dealing with the demands of the time. In England a free public opinion stimulated discussion of public and philosophic questions, while in France censorship and narrow dogmatism stifled the free expression of thought or drove it into subterfuge and excesses.

English Influence. In the spring of 1726 Voltaire, just released from imprisonment in the Bastille, came to

England and stayed there for three years. The impressions he gained there became decisive in his life and, through him, shaped the intellectual development of continental Europe. He was deeply impressed by the freedom of speech which he found in all classes of English society, by the high esteem in which non-aristocrats—scholars, men of letters, and merchants—were held, and by the emphasis on experimental science and practical inventions. In his *Letters Concerning the English Nation* (*see Reading No. 1*) he acquainted the French with English religious tolerance, with the English scientific and empiricist thought from Francis Bacon and Newton to Locke, with the attitude of the British aristocracy to trade and commerce, and with the generally free and fluid social and intellectual life of the island which contrasted so sharply with the rigidity and dogmatism of French life. In his biography of Voltaire, Condorcet wrote that "the example of England showed Voltaire that truth is not meant to remain a secret in the hands of a few philosophers. From this moment on he felt himself called to destroy the prejudices of all kind to which his country was a slave. *Cet ouvrage fit parmi nous l'époque d'une révolution.*" The French historian Pierre Lanfrey called the *Letters* "the eighteenth century work which contributed more new truths than any other book." Thirty years later, on January 16, 1760, Voltaire wrote to an English friend: "Had I not fixed the place of my retreat in the free corner of Geneva, I would certainly live in the free corner of England. I have been for thirty years the disciple of your ways of thinking."

Voltaire and the other philosophers fought for half a century against the authoritarianism, the intolerance, and the censorship of the French church and state. Through these thinkers the English ideas of liberty became known abroad. They were absorbed and transformed into the general consciousness of Western mankind through the genius of French rationalism and the clarity of the French language. "The literature of France," Macaulay pointed out, "has been to ours what Aaron was to Moses, the expositor of great truths which would else have perished for want of a voice to utter them with distinctness. Isolated by our situation, isolated by our manners, we found truth but we did not impart it. France has been the interpreter between England and mankind." Though the moral and political ideas of the Enlightenment were expressed with universal authority and in a language understood by all in France, their practical influence before 1789 was smaller there than in other countries. The French monarchy did not become enlightened, the French censorship remained most oppressive, and religious liberty received no concessions. Toward the end of the eighteenth century, France's official absolutism and dogmatism left her behind other European countries. The gulf separating her traditional government and her enlightened society grew ever wider, as it did a century later in Russia.

The social and intellectual conditions in eighteenth-century France differed fundamentally from those in England. In both countries the middle classes grew in self-confidence, but the English middle class was composed mainly of merchants relying on their own initiative and free enterprise, whereas the French middle class consisted chiefly of lawyers and bureaucrats and looked to the government for support and administrative favors. The new thought both in France and England was rationalist, but there was a significant difference between the broad empiricist approach—the cautious and experimental English realism, which allowed for liberty and diversity—and the abstract and absolutist principles which governed the French mind and which too easily tended to intolerance. French eighteenth-century writers, living like nineteenth-century Russian writers under a despotic régime, did not have to worry about the practical consequences or applicability of their criticisms and suggestions. The influence of public opinion so great in England remained insignificant at the French court. Thus political and intellectual divisions grew more extreme in France than in England. And the bitterness of controversy in France envenomed the debate over religion and church to a degree unknown in England. The attitude toward the church, the institution which embodied religion and Christianity in France, has divided the French nation more permanently in modern times than any other issue and has been closely involved with all the changing political, intellectual and social divisions of modern times. All of these were emotionally colored by the religious or anti-religious implications with which they were closely connected in the French mind.

France Reassumes Leadership. The ideals of the Enlightenment, less well realized in France than elsewhere before 1789, erupted with greater violence as the French attempted to transform them into reality. By this attempt France reassumed the leadership of Europe. The original principles of the French Revolution—the limitation of the power of government, the rights of man and citizen, the removal of impediments to economic progress—had been realized before in a gradual historical process on Europe's western outskirts in England and Anglo-America. But it was the introduction of these principles into the heartland of European civilization, their sudden and apparently spontaneous acceptance among general enthusiasm by a whole people, which filled men everywhere with a new hope and great rejoicing. France recaptured her ascendancy in the minds of men. France, in travail, was setting an example for the world. Thinking men in Europe and the two Americas watched the spectacle in optimistic expectation or uneasy fear. The center of the stage shifted from the Court of Versailles to the People of Paris; the guiding light, from Voltaire to Rousseau.

The two intellectual leaders who exercised the greatest influence in eighteenth-century Europe were both identified with France, though the younger of them came from Calvinist Geneva. They were very different minds. Voltaire fitted into the aristocratic society of his day. He adhered to the classical ideal of France, form and measure, rational thought and ordered clarity. He strove for tolerance and understanding. He wished to influence the course of history through enlightening kings and nobles. Jean-Jacques Rousseau (1712-1778), who had grown up under the freer administration of his native city-republic, wished for a more immediate political regeneration of the world. He turned to the people and aroused their sentiments and combative fervor. To him the state was no longer the court and the educated classes. It was the people, the new sovereign, whose will ought to be as absolute and unified as the king's will had been, though much more difficult to express and demanding far greater efforts to enlighten.

A new temper appeared in the French Revolution. The English and the American revolutions were events of predominantly local importance. They were fundamentally conservative revolutions concerned with the preservation and extension of historical rights and liberties. The French Revolution grew out of a feeling for the need of a total renovation of life and society. It was an event of universal impact and recognized itself as such. It thought of itself as a beginning, concluding a period of mankind, starting, like Christianity, a new chapter in the history of the world.

The Revolution's Universal Appeal. No one expressed the universal appeal of the French Revolution better than the aged German philosopher, Immanuel Kant in far-off Königsberg. He saw it as the supreme fruit of the Enlightenment, "man's emergence from his immaturity, an immaturity for which he himself was responsible. Immaturity is the inability to use one's own intelligence without other guidance. One bears the responsibility for this immaturity if its cause is not the lack of intelligence but the lack of resolution and courage, to use it without other guides. *Sapere aude!* Dare to use your own intelligence! That is the motto of the Enlightenment." The Revolution dared both to think and to act. It combined the intelligence of confident reason that Voltaire represented, with the resolution and courage of stout hearts that Rousseau had called for. This union, which existed only as an ideal conception, provoked, according to Kant, the moral enthusiasm of man. "The revolution of a civilized people, which we have witnessed in our day, may succeed or it may fail; it may be filled with misery and horror to such a degree that a right-thinking man would not decide, if he could hope to make it succeed at a later time, to make the experiment at such tremendous costs; nevertheless, such a revolution arouses in the minds of all spectators (who are not involved themselves) a desire to participate, one which almost verges on enthusiasm, and which, as its expression was dangerous, could therefore have no other cause than a moral faculty in mankind." Kant foresaw the Revolution's far-reaching effects: "For such an event is too great, too closely interwoven with the interest of mankind, and in its influence too widely spread to all parts of the globe to be easily forgotten by the peoples, if favorable circumstances should make new experiments of this kind possible."

The Revolution's National Importance. Kant, the son of the rationalist and universalist Enlightenment, saw only one aspect of the Revolution. He looked on it from without. Its newly aroused militant nationalism escaped him. In its full aspect the Revolution was, above all, a French event. It wished to strengthen and modernize the French state, to restore its efficiency, to solve its financial and economic problems. Its initial success invigorated the French nation. It provided it with a new spirit and new institutions, and thus gave it the confidence to renew its hegemonial aspirations, as she had done in the seventeenth century. Once more France was to lead Europe, politically and culturally. The Revolution went in its enthusiasm beyond the more rational and limited ambitions of Richelieu and Louis XIV. Seen as a whole, from Valmy to Waterloo, the Revolution was an attempt to assert France as the modern Rome. Originally it strove for a renascence of the patriotic and military virtues of the Roman Republic and its proud traditions of liberty-loving citizenship. Later, Napoleon looked upon himself as the restorer of the Roman Empire or at least as a second Charlemagne. In their enthusiasm the French in 1793 went even beyond Rome: they saw Paris as the new Jerusalem, the heavenly city, brought down to earth in order to realize a perfect society in the Ile de France, whence the new gospel of true liberty would spread over the earth. But a few years later the original intoxication had worn off; for Napoleon did not share this messianic faith. He despised ideologues and dreamers. Akin to the great Italian princes of fortune of the Renaissance, he believed in the supreme reality of power and concentrated on the state as an efficient machine built and controlled by a virtuoso.

Yet dreamers and realists alike failed. Neither the

new Rome nor the new Jerusalem were of any duration. The tremendous crisis of France and Europe lasted for twenty-seven years. France's hegemonial attempts were defeated, but they left her exhausted by an effort well beyond her actual strength. Never again was France to achieve the political and military leadership she had exercised in the seventeenth century. After Waterloo the balance of power shifted in her disfavor. Other countries surpassed her in manpower and economic development.

Yet the French Revolution, from Valmy to Waterloo, has never ceased to determine the thought of modern France. The memories of the *jour de gloire* have haunted her; the *enfants de la patrie* have continued to feel themselves the guardians of *la Grande Nation*. But the French Revolution also split French society in an ever-renewed and often embittered debate. Did the Revolution not fail as the kings had failed? When had French history reached its high point and the best foundation for its duration? Was it in the ordered society under the guidance of the great monarchs and the church, from St. Louis to Louis XIV? Or was it in the enthusiasm of August, 1789, and in the ranks of the sansculottes who defeated the armies of the eighteenth-century kings? Or perhaps in the glories of Marengo and Austerlitz and in the spirit of the Code Napoleon which set the law for progressive Europe? French thought for the last 150 years has been preoccupied with debating the value of the French Revolution and its place in French history. Were the Enlightenment and the ensuing Revolution France's greatest achievements, or did they mark the moral and spiritual decline of France, compared with the *ancien régime* from the thirteenth to the seventeenth centuries? The question has been left unanswered.

There have been few Frenchmen indeed in modern times who have not opposed the one France to the other. The French nation as a whole has never accepted the French Revolution in the same way as the English accepted the Glorious Revolution or the Americans their Constitution—as a definite settlement, binding all classes and traditions in a common loyalty. Since 1792 France has been split into two camps, and this fact has turned French history into a succession of revolutions and coun-

ter-revolutions, changing constitutions, and open or latent
civil wars. The antagonism between parties and classes,
much sharper than in English-speaking countries, created
an inner tension which contributed to France's political
and social weakness. But this ever-acute tension also
stimulated French intellectual life. Modern political
theories were nowhere defined with as much incisiveness
and awareness as in nineteenth-century France. In this
intellectually exciting atmosphere arts and letters were
thriving. Though France's political and military leadership declined irretrievably in the nineteenth century, her
cultural influence remained unimpaired. The modern
French mind reflected the general problems of the
European continent and its changing intellectual moods
with exemplary clarity and insight. For that reason, in
spite of her declining material power, France's prestige
remained unique. More than ever have Europeans in
modern times regarded France as their second fatherland,
and Paris as their intellectual home.

— 2 —

FAITH AND REASON

Reason and Liberty. The eighteenth century is
known as the Age of Reason, of confidence in man's
unlimited capacity to guide his own conduct and to build
a perfect society. The progress of science revealed the
power of the mind to penetrate the secrets of nature. It
made it clear that the universe obeys natural laws intelligible to human understanding. Might not the progress of
science perform similar feats in the realm of social and

personal behavior and thereby put the life of societies and
nations on the rational basis of general and intelligible
laws? Would such laws not set men free from arbitrary
powers and past superstitions and thus assure his limitless
progress? These hopes of the century found their noblest
expression in the *Outlines of the Historical View of the
Progress of the Human Mind* by the Marquis de Condorcet (1743-1794).

By his noble birth and by his great achievement as a
mathematician, Condorcet occupied a high position in the
society of the *ancien régime*. Yet during the Revolution
he joined the republicans and voted for the death of the
king. His opposition to the Terror, however, forced him
into hiding. There, under the shadow of death, he wrote
the supreme declaration of faith in man's power to effect
infinite progress through his reason. (*See Reading No. 2.*)
Condorcet saw mankind, emancipated from its chains,
released alike from the dominion of chance and of enmity
to man's progress, advancing with a firm and undeviating
step in the path of truth. This vision was the asylum into
which he retired and whither no persecutors could
follow him. He forgot his own misfortunes in feeling at
one with those wiser and happier beings of the future
whose enviable condition he was so earnestly endeavoring to bring about. In Condorcet and countless others,
the faith in reason and liberty found heroes and martyrs
equal to those of any other faith.

The growing faith in reason, from Voltaire to Condorcet, challenged the traditional Christian view of the nature of man. The Christian doctrine of original sin was
replaced by the eighteenth-century doctrine of the natural
goodness and perfectibility of man. Trust in salvation
through Christ and the supernatural powers of the
church gave way to confidence in man's salvation by
the progress of reason. The belief in society superseded
the belief in divinity, or, perhaps more accurately, society
and divinity were equated. To serve one's nation or mankind meant to serve God. Soon again the individual's
liberty and happiness were immolated on the altar of the
new divinity. To Voltaire's concern for liberty and reform
was added the Rousseauan craving for the perfect community of equal beings. The new faith turned into a

church of its own, complete with dogmatic infallibility and the enforcement of its own way of salvation.

The Perfect Society. Voltaire wished to enlighten kings; Rousseau desired to work with the aroused passions of the human heart. Voltaire appealed to reason; Rousseau to human nature. Rousseau could do it because as an eighteenth-century man he was convinced that nature was good and the manifestation of reason itself. Only the nineteenth-century romanticists dissociated human nature from reason and goodness. Baudelaire and Dostoevsky saw the dark abyss in the human soul. But Rousseau's disciples, Maximilien Robespierre (1758-1794) and Louis Antoine Léon de Saint-Just (1767-1794), were convinced that "man is good by nature; whosoever denies this principle cannot think of putting man into his rightful place. If man is corrupted, the vices of social institutions are responsible for it. If nature has made man good, we have to bring him back to nature." The perfect state would be the one in accord with the natural virtuousness of man. Any opposition to such a state or to the laws of virtue must be regarded as unnatural and treasonous. The eighteenth-century social theory emphasized the harmony of nature, and Rousseau, an idyllic pacifist, thought the same. Robespierre and Saint-Just represented the transition from the belief in pre-ordained harmony to the ruthless struggle for the realization of the idea.

Saint-Just began his indictment of Danton, saying, "There is something terrible in the sacred love of the fatherland. This love is so exclusive that it sacrifices everything to the public interest, without pity, without fear, with no respect for the human individual." Robespierre and his Jacobin followers accepted Rousseau's theory of the general will. This will must be one and indivisible, a sovereign authority which does not tolerate any opposition or deviation. This absolutism of the will of the people was readily adopted by the French revolutionists because it was in agreement with French tradition. Robespierre's generation grew up in Jesuit schools, imbued with spiritual and political authoritarianism; nor were the models of Sparta and Rome conducive to an understanding of liberty and tolerance or of the intricacies of free discussion and patient inquiry. To the new French patriot, as the French historian Albert Sorel pointed out, liberty was identical with unlimited sovereignty. "This attitude was called Roman liberty, and this conception, renewed by Rousseau and his entire school, adapted itself marvellously to the classical formula, for a long time approved in France by the monarchy. It belongs to the French way of life and tradition. For some, this Roman pride went hand in hand with force of character and the most valiant steadfastness of the soul: they fought for their principles, succumbed with a stoic faith or retired with dignity after defeat of their party. For the others, the great majority, it was above all a pride of State, jealous and suspicious of competitors, implacable to the defeated, arrogant toward foreigners, but perfectly pliable to force and extremely capable of reconciling itself to submission to a master, whoever he might be, a crowd, a faction, a dictator, a general, the People or the Committee, Robespierre or Bonaparte." This liberty had nothing in common with the liberty understood in England or by Voltaire.

The Civic Religion. Robespierre, a young provincial lawyer, was deputy from Paris in the National Convention. On July 27, 1793, he became the leading member of the Committee of Public Safety, a position which he held until his downfall on 9 Thermidor (July 28), 1794. He used his power not only to save France and the Revolution but also to realize his ideas of public virtue and civic religion. The Terror associated with his name had a moral goal, to crush the enemies of the perfect ethical order of equality and liberty and thus to assure its speedy advent. Around him, Robespierre saw fallible mankind; yet he was convinced that the Revolution could free men from their egoistic passions and dedicate them to patriotic virtue. "Virtue!" he exclaimed on July 26, 1794, "It is without doubt the natural passion, but how could these venal souls accessible only to dastardly and savage passions know it? But it exists, I swear, O sensitive and pure souls, it exists, this tender, imperious, irresistible passion, torment and delight of magnanimous hearts! This profound horror of tyranny, this compassionate zeal for the oppressed, this sacred

love of mankind, without which a great revolution is but
a startling crime, destroying an earlier crime; it exists,
that generous ambition to found on earth the first
republic of the world!" These were Robespierre's feelings
two days before his downfall and execution.

Robespierre had as lofty an idea of the French people
as he had of man. The generation of the French Revolution saw at once the abstractions, Man, Citizen, Nation—
all obeying the same laws of development—and the
specific nature and position of the French people. In May
1794, speaking on the relationship of moral ideas and
republican principles, Robespierre was "tempted to consider the French people who seemed to be 2000 years
ahead of the rest of the human species, an altogether
different breed. In Europe, the laborer and the artisan
are mere animals raised to provide pleasure for the
noblemen. In France, the aristocrats are trying to become laborers and artisans, and they have not been able
to obtain this honor." Such a complete overturn of
society could not be sustained without a new faith.
Robespierre objected to Voltaire and the philosophers
because they never proclaimed the full rights of the
people and because they shared the skeptical and ma-
terialist concepts of the aristocratic society of their time.
Robespierre proclaimed "the idea of a Supreme Being
and of the immortality of the soul, which constitutes an
everlasting appeal to justice," and which was therefore
"a social and republican idea," whereas the religion of
the priests resembled atheism. The priests banished God
to heaven as to a faraway royal palace and recalled him
to earth only to help them demand tithes, riches, power,
and pleasures for their own benefit. But the new faith
was different. It was this-worldly, virtuous and devoted to
the people's happiness. "Nature is the true priest of the
Supreme Being, the universe is His Temple," Robespierre
proclaimed. "One can worship him only with virtue. His
festivals consist of the happiness of a great people,
assembled before Him, in order to tighten the gentle
bonds of universal brotherhood and to render Him
homage with their pure and sensitive hearths." (*See
Reading No. 3.*)

The Terror.   Saint-Just was a puritan zealot in the

service of the new faith. "The pure love of the fatherland is the only foundation of liberty. There cannot be any liberty in a nation where consideration for the glamour of wealth plays any part. One can build a republic only by frugality and virtue. What can there be in common between glory and wealth?" Men had to be taught to "bear with docility the yoke of public happiness," to become indissolubly united in the fellowship of virtue, to abandon all their private interests and passions to the total service of the one sovereign people. On October 10, 1793, Saint-Just defined the principle of terror as the rejection of all lukewarmness, all indifference, all life not fully engaged in the common weal: "You have to punish not only the traitors, but even those who are indifferent. You have to punish whoever is passive in the Republic and does nothing for it. Since the French people manifested its will, everything opposed to it is outside the sovereign. Whatever is outside the sovereign is an enemy."

The Terror of the French Revolution, which threw its shadow in France over the June 1848 days and over the Paris Commune, was in itself short-lived. Only in Russia after 1917, in an entirely different intellectual atmosphere, did terror become a permanent institution. In France, Robespierre himself was eager to terminate it the very same day when he and Saint-Just were arrested. Even in the days of the Terror there was no single party dominating the country or the parliamentary assembly. The Committee of Public Safety never fully controlled the Convention, nor did Robespierre ever fully control the Committee. The Convention in France soon grew disgusted with exaltation, bloodshed, and exceptional laws. It restored some of the liberties of 1789. Even the régime of Napoleon Bonaparte, which again destroyed these liberties, never returned to terrorism. Yet the short-lived Terror with its jealous God of intolerant civic religion, its quest for the mystical general will of the nation and for a perfect society, has haunted French history and thought to the present. The extremism of hopes and fears aroused by these memories has led to bitter and continuous domestic factionalism.

Napoleon. Five years after Robespierre's fall an-

other individual claimed to embody the general will of
the sovereign French people, General Napoleon Bonaparte (1769-1821). Robespierre's ideal was a democracy,
expressing itself not in parliamentary factions or in the
clash and compromise of interests, but in an ever-
renewed enthusiastic popular plebiscite. Napoleon replaced this *démocratie plébiscitaire* by a *césarisme plébiscitaire,* an authoritarian régime which was to prevent
factionalism and to express the general will, and which
received its legitimacy from popular acclaim. The ascendancy of a victorious general was prepared by the prestige
of the republican army, whose successes had endeared it
to the French people. Napoleon, like Robespierre, appealed to an exalted patriotism, a militant pride alien to
the spirit of the Glorious Revolution, of Locke and
Voltaire. But, on one decisive point, Napoleon's rule
differed radically from that of Robespierre. Napoleon was
an eighteenth-century enlightened despot, therein much
more in the tradition of Voltaire than in that of Rousseau. In his unification of France, his centralized administration, his legal codes, his educational reforms,
the enlightened rationalism of the middle of the century
in which Napoleon was born gained its final triumph.
Napoleon was defeated not only by the hubris of his
ambition—in which he more greatly resembled the
Faustian man of the Renaissance than the eighteenth-
century rationalist—but by popular forces which the
French Revolution had aroused abroad and which the
eighteenth-century rationalist could not comprehend.

Napoleon as a personality influenced French and
European thought by the uniqueness of his achievement.
Here was a man before whom Pope and kings alike
bowed, who disposed of crowns and destinies at will; and
this man had reached his supreme position through his
strength and daring alone, unsupported by any tradition
or birthright. When, after his fall, France and Europe
settled into the quietude of the Restoration period, a
Napoleonic legend emerged. The memory of the heroic
epopee stirred many youth into a feeling of greatness,
contrasting with the alleged smallness of the time. Napoleon became the idol of many Romanticists in their
quest for the self-realization of the unique and great

personality. Napoleon as a prisoner and "martyr" at St. Helena helped to create the legend. He interpreted his life and intentions, making himself appear as the unifier of Europe and the guardian of the liberties of the people against royal absolutism and mob violence. There were poets and intellectuals in continental Europe who contrasted the heroic legend which centered around Napoleon to the "shopkeeper mentality" of England which had defeated Napoleon and kept him cruelly imprisoned. The anonymous forces of modern middle-class society and of Anglo-American parliamentarianism appeared unintelligible and therefore suspect; their rejection frequently found expression in the desire for a visible and personal authority, a man on horseback, an embodiment of the people's will.

Revival of Traditionalism.   Beside the Terror and the legend of Napoleon, other past memories exercised their influence on French thought. After 1800 the days before 1789 appeared filled with gentleness and sweetness; nostalgically some men began to turn their minds backward. The French Revolution and its aftermath had caused a breakdown of French society and thought. Great hopes had been frustrated, there was general insecurity, and unending wars had brought chaos and misery. Experience had disproved an abundance of brilliant theories. It is no wonder that in the quest for social order and a secure faith, the *ancien régime,* the aristocracy, and the church began to appear to some in a new light. François René Vicomte de Chateaubriand (1768-1848), "the most conspicuous figure in French literature during the First Empire," wrote an essay in 1797 containing a chapter which asked, "What religion will replace Christianity?" The answer seemed no longer in doubt five years later, when he published *Le Génie du Christianisme,* a book which immediately established his fame. Its sub-title, "The Beauty of the Christian Religion," expressed the spirit of the book. Christianity was returning triumphantly, and Chateaubriand opened the work with a quotation from Montesquieu: "How admirable is the Christian religion whose sole object seems to be our bliss in the life thereafter and which yet gives us happiness here and now."

The lyrical mood of the book met the post-revolutionary need for comfort and sweetness. The world had become uglier since the Revolution. The Revolution had failed to regenerate man. Was mankind not steeped in blood and sin? Chateaubriand's hero, René, used to watch the serenity on the face of penitent sinners in churches. "Ah!" he cried. "Who has not sometimes felt the need of self-regeneration, the need to steep his soul anew in the fountain of life? Who does not sometimes feel crushed by the burden of his own corruption and incapable of doing anything great, noble or just?" But regeneration could no longer come, as Robespierre had thought, from Nature and Reason. Could not the church with its ages-old serene beauty restore the harmony of a distracted world? "The degenerate world calls for a second preaching of the Gospel. Christianity undergoes a renovation and emerges victorious from the most terrible attack which hell ever launched against it. Who knows whether what we regard as the fall of the Church is not its rebuilding? The Church perished in its wealth and lassitude. It no longer remembered the Cross. The Cross has reappeared, the Church will be saved."

Chateaubriand longed for a reformed Christianity, compatible with liberty and progress. (*See Readings Nos. 4, 5.*) Like so many of his generation he felt that he belonged to two different worlds, to two different ages. He did not wish wholly to restore the past, nor did he share the unconditional faith in the future. In the very name of reason he protested against the radical revolutionary attempts to change the form of government. "I, too, would like to spend my days under the democratic régime of my dreams, for, in theory, democracy is the best form of government. Perhaps my present opinions can be explained as the triumph of reason over natural inclinations. To pretend that republics could be created everywhere, despite all obstacles, is preposterous and at times even wicked." In his last work, looking back on his life, he wrote: "Along spiritual lines I wanted to give religion and liberty to my country, along temporal lines I wanted to bring her honor and glory. I found myself in two centuries, at the junction of two roads. I plunged into troubled waters, regretfully leaving the old shore where I was born, hopefully swimming toward a new and unknown shore. . . . While writing these last words, at six o'clock in the morning, I see the pale moon expanding as she sinks behind the spire of the Invalides which has just come into view with the first rays of the sun. One would think that the old world has ended and that the new world has just begun. I see the reflections of the first light of day, but I will never see the sun rise. All that is left to me is to sit at the edge of the pit; thereafter I will bravely descend into eternity with a crucifix in my hand."

Faith and Order.   Chateaubriand wished to build a bridge between two ages. His fellow aristocrats, Joseph Comte de Maistre (1753-1821) and Louis Gabriel Ambroise, Vicomte de Bonald (1754-1840), insisted upon an unconditional return to the *ancien régime*. In their systems there was no room for modern liberty. In 1797 both published refutations of the French Revolution which they condemned as essentially satanic. Both regarded the authoritarian church and the absolute monarchy as the only possible foundation of the political, social and cultural order of a unified Europe which would find its center in a papal theocracy. Maistre rejected not only Rousseau but regarded Voltaire as the embodiment of wickedness. "Nothing can absolve him. His corruption is in a class by itself; it is rooted in the deepest fibres of his heart and fortified by all the powers of his intelligence. With a fury which is unequalled in this world, this insolent blasphemer, from the depths of his nothingness, dares to call the Saviour of mankind a ridiculous name and to call the divine law infamous." Maistre's work was a radical challenge to the most cherished beliefs of the Enlightenment: he went so far as to proclaim the executioner the cornerstone of the social edifice and war a divine institution. (*See Reading No. 6.*) Maistre and Bonald pinned their hopes upon the Catholic monarchy of France. "Since the time of Charlemagne," Bonald wrote in 1819, "there has always been an authority in Europe which was respected even by its rivals and recognized even by its enemies: the leadership of France. No great political action was ever performed without France. She was the trustee of every

tradition of the great family, and the repository of all
the state secrets of Christendom. I dare to say that no
great act will ever be performed without her; what assures her of this pre-eminence for all time, and to a
degree sets the final seal on it, is the universality of her
language, which has been adopted by cabinets and
courts, and is consequently the language of politics."
Little did Bonald foresee that the age of nationalism
which the French Revolution had engendered would put
an end to the universality of the French language.

Faith and the People. The trends of thought and
hope expressed in the French Revolution invaded even
the Catholic church. Hughes Félicité Robert de Lamennais (1782-1854), a Catholic priest who developed from
a firm supporter of ultra-conservative church authority
to a religious liberal, in 1831 edited a newspaper, charac-
teristically called *L'Avenir*. He did not look back to a
church which would rule men's minds by fear or outward power; rather he looked forward to a future in
which spiritual forces would lead men in perfect freedom. In his *Paroles d'un Croyant* (1834), Lamennais
still clung to the hope that the papacy would support a
reconciliation between the traditional faith and modern
democracy. He dedicated the book to the People. "What
the people wills," he wrote in 1839, "God Himself wills;
for what the people wills is justice, the essential and
eternal order, the fulfillment in mankind of that sublime
word of Christ, 'That they be One, My Father, as You
and I are One.' The cause of the people is therefore the
sacred cause, the cause of God. It will triumph." By this
time Lamennais' hope of papal support for a Christian
democracy had vanished. The encyclical *"Mirari vos"*
had condemned *L'Avenir*. Lamennais broke with the
church. What remained to him was his faith in the
people, in the invisible church of democratic liberty and
human brotherhood. His aspirations merged with the
broad stream of the movement for social regeneration
which swept Restoration France irresistibly toward the
Revolution of 1848.

SOCIAL REGENERATION

Science and Industry. During the French Revolution, François-Noël Babeuf (1760-1797), who changed his first name to Gracchus, tried to carry the tendencies inherent in Robespierre's Jacobinism to their logical conclusion. He agitated for an equalitarian communism and a dictatorship of the "true" nation, a confraternity of the "true" faith. Filippo Michele Buonarroti (1761-1836), a Tuscan who became naturalized in France, transmitted Babeuf's faith to later generations. But this first appearance of an extremist socialism, appealing to the oppressed classes and calling for violence, was of little importance compared with the attempt of Claude Henri de Rouvroy, Comte de Saint-Simon (1760-1825), to save the world from the anarchy of the French Revolution by establishing a new unity of faith and society. He centered his attention not on mass movements but on technical or social organzation. As a youth he had fought in the Battle of Yorktown "for the cause of industrial liberty," as he later said. Saint-Simon shared Condorcet's faith in progress and science, and at the same time Maistre's longing for order and harmonious stability. Yet he rejected the latter's nostalgia for the past, for he knew that there was no way leading backward. He was one of the first men on the continent to envisage the coming of a new order, based upon a cult of science and economic productivity and administered by scientists and technologic experts. He drew the ultimate conclusions from the enthusiasm for science which began with Voltaire's visit to England and characterized the latter half of the French eighteenth century, an enthusiasm which led to the founding of the Institut de France in 1794 and of the École Polytechnique in the following year.

But Saint-Simon went beyond this general enthusiasm

for technological innovations and explorations. He saw in the French Revolution the climax of a profound moral, spiritual and social crisis which had begun with the Renaissance and Reformation. He longed for an age of spiritual and social harmony. He felt the need for a new unified body of knowledge like that of the Middle Ages, as the basis for an integrated society. He was driven, as he wrote in 1812, by "the passion of science and of the public good, by the desire to find a means of terminating in a peaceful way the frightful crisis in which all of European society is involved." Like Maistre, he regarded the eighteenth century as an age of criticism, of the dissolution of old values and creeds. But he thought this century a necessary transition to a new, positive and organic age which would establish the happiness of man on a secure basis.

Saint-Simon interpreted Christianity as a social religion of love and association. This new Christianity proclaimed the brotherhood of man, no longer only in the negative sense of doing unto others as you wish others to do unto you, but in the positive sense that each man must work productively to effect the speediest and fullest improvement of the moral and material existence of the most numerous class, the poor. The road to this improvement lay open in the nineteenth century; it was the application of science to society. The names of the periodicals which he founded or planned, *L'Industrie, L'Organisiteur, Le Producteur,* emphasized productive industry, by which he meant the work of factory owners and laborers, farmers and merchants alike. On them, and not on the old ruling classes, the wealth and progress of the entire nation depended. Therefore the industrialists should take the direction of national life into their hands. He foresaw government by a "technocratic" parliament of three chambers. The first chamber would represent "invention." Composed of scientists, artists and engineers, it would plan the annual program of public works and national festivities. The second chamber, dedicated to "examination," was to consist of scientists who would examine the projects proposed by the first chamber and supervise national education. Finally, a third chamber, composed of leaders of industry, would execute the decisions of the other chambers and control the budget.

Utopian Socialism. Saint-Simon was no revolutionary and no democrat. Though he felt the urgency of reform, he relied upon reason and persuasion; and he believed in the authoritarian leadership of a new élite, composed of scientists who represented the new priesthood, and leaders of industry who formed the new aristocracy. Yet in his attempt to establish a new "organic age," he failed as completely as did de Maistre. De Maistre's reactionary dream of the restoration of the leadership of priesthood and aristocracy vanished in 1830 with the advent of the middle-class régime of Louis Philippe and with the revival of the spirit of Voltaire. Saint-Simon's progressive utopia likewise was never realized. The nineteenth century did not become an organic age like the Middle Ages. It remained a "critical" age, an age of rapid changes and contradictory beliefs, of insecurity and vanishing faith. Science was not able to supply a universally accepted basis of a new faith and a new society, a body of undisputed beliefs which could take the place of religion. But Saint-Simon's teaching captivated the imagination of young Europe to a degree which de Maistre's influence never reached. De Maistre was entirely out of feeling with the temper of the nineteenth century. Saint-Simon became the theoretical spokesman of the rapid rise of industry and technology.

After Saint-Simon's death, some enthusiastic disciples under the leadership of Barthélemy Prosper Enfantin (1796-1864) perverted Saint-Simonism into a sectarian religion which preached the complete emancipation of women and of the flesh. The movement collapsed within one decade. Yet the influence of Saint-Simon's ideas remained and was not confined to France or to his generation. Many of the promoters of the industrial revolution in the France of the Second Empire were his disciples. John Stuart Mill in his autobiography recalled that Saint-Simonism had modified his utilitarian individualism. Together with François Fourier (1772-1837), Saint-Simon became the inspiration of the early socialist ideas and movements in countries as far apart as Russia and the United States. Saint-Simon taught that politics should be a science of production; work, the fountainhead of all virtue; and the state, a confederacy of all producers. (*See Readings Nos. 7, 8.*)

Franco-British Unity. Saint-Simon attracted as his secretaries two young men of great promise, Augustin Thierry (1795-1856), who became a well known historian, and Auguste Comte (1798-1857), who was to continue and transform his master's scientific positivism. Saint-Simon foresaw not only the social and organizational consequences of an industrial society: his fertile mind anticipated future forms of international organization as well. Together with Thierry, he submitted, in October 1814, a proposal for "The Reorganization of European Society." He believed that after the dissolution of European society by the French Revolution, a return to former international anarchy was impossible. Industrial society demanded the preservation of peace and the securing of liberty. To that end, the peoples of Europe had to be united in a single body politic while preserving for each their national independence. As the cornerstone of a free Europe, Saint-Simon suggested the closest collaboration between Britain and France; since they were both liberal and parliamentary states, they could form the nucleus of a European federation dedicated to the preservation of peace and the spread of liberty. The self-interest of the two nations demanded such a step: only a Franco-British union could end the turmoil and ills of French society and guide it in the ways of liberty and order. Britain had behind her 130 years of the parliamentary government upon which the French were only now embarking; the constitutional parties in France could find support in Britain against the domestic threats both of despotism and of an extravagant liberty.

Therefore Saint-Simon asked for a solemn declaration on the part of the French nation: "That the English people by the conformity of our institutions with its own, by that affinity of principles and that community of social interests which are the strongest ties between men, is henceforth our natural ally, and that the interest of the whole of Europe demands that the Anglo-French union be rendered more intimate, stronger and more regular, by an accord between the two governments." Thus, Saint-

Simon anticipated by 125 years the proposal of Franco-British union which the British government under Winston Churchill submitted to the French government in June, 1940; it was the tragedy of France and of the Western world that in 1919 the British (and Americans) and in 1940 the French rejected such a close tie-up of France and the English-speaking peoples. Saint-Simon and Thierry went so far as to demand the formation of an Anglo-French parliament, composed of two-thirds English and one-third French deputies. As the reason for this curious proportion they adduced the fact that "the French are still inexperienced in parliamentary politics and need to be under the guidance of the trained and experienced English," and that in entering the union, England would make a greater sacrifice while France would gain more by acquiring the stability and liberty which she lacked.

Positivist Humanism. Thierry, after separating from Saint-Simon, became the historian of the development and rise of the French middle class, the *Tiers Etat.* Comte followed Saint-Simon in desiring a positive and constructive new order which would solve the social problems through the methods of science. His Catholic and Royalist family background and his training as a mathematician may explain the spirit of strict hierarchy and mathematical symmetry which pervades his *Cours de Philosophie Positive,* which he published in six volumes from 1830 to 1842. There he established a hierarchy of sciences, starting with mathematics and ascending through astronomy, physics, chemistry, and biology to the new science of sociology which he founded and which he ranked highest because it deals with mankind and not, as biology does, with man. The new age, which Comte called "the age of positivism," he regarded as an age of maturity and realism, leaving behind the infantile stages of theological and metaphysical speculation. He expected his philosophy of positive science to end the political and intellectual anarchy of the transitional age and thus to re-establish, on a higher level, the harmony of society and thought as it existed in medieval Christianity.

Soon Comte began to regard himself as the founder of a new religion which would exercise a spiritual authority similar to that formerly wielded by the church. The new religion replaced the idea of God with the idea of mankind, and the priests with positivist scientists. Humanity was *le grand être,* the Great Being; its cult was directed not so much to adore it as to improve it. In 1852 Comte published his *Catechism of Positivism* or *Summary and Exposition of the Universal Religion.* The slogans which served as mottoes were "Order and Progress" and "Love as our principle, Order as our basis, Progress as our end." The new religion and the new priesthood were to be as uncompromising as the preceding churches. "In the name of the Past and the Future, the servants of Humanity, both its philosophical and its practical servants, come forward to claim as their due the general direction of this work. Their object is to constitute at length a real Providence in all fields, moral, intellectual and material. Consequently, they exclude, once and for all, from political supremacy, all the different servants of God—Catholic, Protestant or Deist—as being at once obsolete and a cause of disturbance." Comte's scheme for the social reorganization of mankind was indifferent to the ideals of a free society. (*See Reading No. 9.*) The main current of nineteenth-century French thought accepted many of Comte's goals—a humanist secularism, social progress, the organization of mankind for peace. It rejected his absolutist and dogmatic methods. But, in the middle of the nineteenth century, impatience with existing conditions, the shocking and widespread misery of the working class, the romantic penchant for sweeping solutions, led many others to demand and expect a total social regeneration.

Humanitarian Socialism. Some of the most popular writers of the age participated in the agitation. The great poet Victor Hugo (1802-1885) celebrated the revolution in his commemoration of the fifth anniversary of February 1848: "May the next revolution be invincible! May it found the United States of Europe! May it, like February, redeem and place upon its altar, the tripod, liberty, equality, fraternity. May it enkindle on this tripod the great flame of humanity, enlightening the whole earth." The poet Alphonse de Lamartine (1790-1869) pursued his humanitarian ideals as a statesman. He was a member of the Chamber of Deputies from 1833 on and head of the provisional government established in the Revolution of February 1848. He put his poetry into the service of the poor and of peace. "The question today," he wrote in *Des Destinées de la Poesie* (1834), "is not merely whether power shall pass from royalty to the people. The question is deeper than that: We have to decide whether the ethical idea, the religious idea, the idea of evangelical charity shall replace selfishness in politics." The popular novelist George Sand (1803-1876), in her quest for a "religious and social truth, one and the same," collaborated closely with Pierre Leroux (1797-1871), who believed in democracy as a religion, ultimately to be established on a world scale. No less a man than Renan described the enormous impression that George Sand made on her generation: "Her works are truly the echo of our age, and she will be loved when this age is no more. Her books will forever be a witness of all that we have hoped for, thought, felt and suffered." Leroux and Louis Blanc (1813-1882) agreed in regarding universal suffrage as an instrument of social regeneration, and thought or ideas as the dominant force in history.

Revolutionary Socialism. Much nearer to the tradition of Babeuf and Buonarroti was Louis Auguste Blanqui (1805-1881). He stressed action not thought. He believed in conspiracy. He joined the revolutionary movement at the age of eighteen, and of the following fifty-eight years, he spent almost thirty-four in jail and almost ten in exile. But the most truly French of all the early Socialists was Pierre Joseph Proudhon (1809-1865), who is generally known as an anarchist or libertarian and is famed for the answer which he gave to his own question: "What is property?" "Property is theft." He combined a Jacobin passion for justice with a Voltairean love for liberty.

In opposition to Rousseau and to the socialist trend of his own time, Proudhon stressed individual freedom, competition and balance, against political authoritarianism and economic collectivism. He rejected alike the fatalism of historical and theological systems. He recognized the danger in the absolutization of any idea. "I have no system, I will have none, and I expressly repudiate the suggestion. Whatever the system of humanity is, it will only be known when humanity has come to its end. . . . All ideas are false when one endows them with an exclusive and absolute meaning or when one allows oneself to be swept away by this meaning." On May 17, 1846, Proudhon warned Karl Marx in a letter: "Let us not in our turn think of indoctrinating the people after having demolished all *a priori* dogmas. Let us not fall into the contradiction of your compatriot Luther, who, after having overturned Catholic theology, set out immediately, with many anathemas of his own, to found a Protestant theology." In the midst of the enthusiasm and confusion of 1848-1849, he wrote that "what our generation needs is not a Mirabeau, a Robespierre or a Bonaparte, but a Voltaire. Liberty, like reason, exists and manifests itself only by continuing contempt of its own works; it perishes when it descends to self-adoration. All solemn peoples are stationary peoples." Looking at the condition of France more than a decade later, he found little cause for hope. "Is it the need for authority that is making itself felt everywhere, or is it a disgust with independence, or only an incapacity for self-government?"

Was the people, so enraptured with liberty in 1789, growing weary of it? In the 1860s the picture seemed dark. The new synthesis of faith and reason, of liberty and order, had not been found. Industrialization had made great progress under Napoleon III, but there could be no doubt that social regeneration had not been achieved nor the tradition of liberty firmly accepted. France had tried to revive all the three legends of its past grandeur: that of the absolute monarchy and an authoritarian church, under Charles X; that of the revolutions of 1789 and 1793, in February and June 1848; and finally, the legend of Napoleon, in the patriotic fever of 1840, when Napoleon's remains were triumphantly brought home from St. Helena, and in the ascent of Louis Napoleon to the renewed imperial throne. All three legends failed France. The Restoration Monarchy, the Second Republic, the Second Empire—all had ended in equal disaster. The optimism of 1848 was gone. After a turmoil of eighty years, neither the political nor the social problems seemed near a settlement. "We shall not live to see the new age," Proudhon wrote a few years before his death; "we shall fight in the darkness. We must prepare ourselves to endure this life without too much sadness by doing our duty. Let us help one another, call to one another in the gloom, and practice justice wherever opportunity offers."

In the midst of this disillusionment, a greater realism, a better understanding of history, was growing. Liberty was no longer claimed as the natural birthright of man, but recognized as a precarious and ever-threatened possession, secured only by ceaseless effort. Nor could an era of perfect happiness be expected. In notes to his novel *Les Misérables,* Victor Hugo made it clear that social regeneration had its limits. Society can progressively and slowly do away with poverty and destitution, but it has little power over suffering. "Suffering, we deeply believe, is the law of this earth, until some new Divine dispensation."

— 4 —

THE LIBERAL TRADITION

"Liberty" and the Liberal Tradition.   French history from 1789 to the present day can be divided into two almost equal periods. From 1789 to 1875 revolutions and counter-revolutions followed each other in quick succession. Régimes of liberty were always threatened and often superseded by dictatorships. In this period liberalism existed as a doctrine and a program, but there was no liberal tradition. Neither the monarchy of the seventeenth and eighteenth centuries nor the Revolution and

Napoleon had prepared France for a liberal régime. "Liberty" was a rational demand, not a way of life. In 1858 Ernest Renan warned the French against a "liberalism, which pretends to base itself on the principles of reason alone and thinks it does not need tradition. This is its error. The liberal school erred in believing that it is easy to create liberty by reasoning alone. It did not recognize that enduring liberty can spring only from historical roots." Liberty had grown from historical roots in England; there the liberal tradition had become deeply ingrained in the public mind in the course of more than two centuries.

In France, liberty had suddenly burst forth in 1789. For the following decades the word became an article of faith, enthusiastically adored or utterly damned. Without regard for the realities behind the word, people liked to call themselves "sincere friends of liberty" or to assure themselves and their audiences of their "passion for liberty," much as "democracy" and "peace-loving" have been invoked since 1945. "Liberty" and the liberal tradition turned out to have little in common. When Louis Napoleon (1808-1873) extolled the reign of his uncle, whom he intended to imitate, he praised "love of liberty" as the essence of the Napoleonic reign. (*See Reading No. 11.*) But the Spaniards and the Tyrolese, the Russians and the Prussians, who fought Napoleon's "tyranny," also professed themselves motivated by "love of liberty." Yet there was as little liberty in Spain or Tyrol, Russia or Prussia as there was under Napoleon. In fact, it can be said that Napoleon's rule exercised liberating influences abroad. His armies aroused the peoples of Europe from lethargy and brought them new principles of law and administration. In France, however, Napoleon's régime exalted dictatorship instead of individual liberties and the mystical will of the nation instead of the free interplay of forces. Napoleon's administrative centralization condemned all local self-government. Military triumphs and patriotic passions proved inimical to the growth of liberty. The Napoleonic heritage was as heavy a mortgage on the nascent liberal tradition in France as the Terror.

Constant Warns the French. Napoleonic France

had been defeated by the coöperation of the liberal West and the autocratic East. After 1815 France had the choice of aligning herself with the liberal and commercialized West, thus making possible the growth of a liberal tradition, or of continuing her policy of heroic glory, placing herself between the East and West. Benjamin Constant (1767-1830) warned the French in his *De l'Esprit de conquête et de l'usurpation dans leurs rapports avec la civilisation Européenne* (1814) against the spirit of military glory, an ancient and hallowed spirit, but one opposed to modern Western civilization. This modern civilization was animated by the "commercial instinct," the instinct of peace, prevailing over "that narrow and hostile emotion which people cover with the name of patriotism." War, Constant wrote, is a savage and passionate impulse; commerce on the other hand, a civilized and rational calculation. He denounced military dictatorship and the longing for national uniformity, which inevitably must lead to the loss of liberty, not only in the conquered countries but at home. Under Napoleon, the whole of Europe had become a vast prison, deprived of all communication "with that noble country, England, the generous asylum of free thought, the illustrious refuge for the dignity of the human race." In an open letter to Chateaubriand, Constant pleaded for moderation, against recrimination and vengefulness in political life: "You must show you want freedom for all by claiming it on behalf of those with whom you disagree. You must admit that while certain scoundrels committed dreadful deeds during the last twenty-seven years of our history, yet men of all parties gave magnificent examples of disinterestedness and courage. You must not exclude from power all those who served Bonaparte or the republic, for those men are virtually the whole of France. We must neither ignore the past and take it as an episode in our history to be forgotten as quickly as possible, nor see in any one past period the whole of our history."

Constant called for moderation as a guide for foreign and domestic policy. He cited the civilian society of England, its cult of legality, and its habit of compromise, as a model. Military nations like the French, he wrote, did not understand the strength of such a society. "They regarded weakness as ignoble, laws as superfluous subtleties, and they despised parliamentary procedures for their allegedly unbearable slowness. They preferred rapid and trenchant decisions as in a war and believed unanimity of opinion as essential as in an army. They regarded opposition as disorder, critical reasoning as revolt, the courts as military tribunals, the judges as soldiers who must execute the orders of the authority. Those who were suspect or accused, they viewed as if they were enemies or convicted criminals, and they considered the judgment of the courts as battles in the state of war into which they had transformed the government." In this analysis of Revolutionary and Napoleonic France, Constant anticipated the totalitarian governments of the twentieth century. He decried Rousseau's general will as "the evil ally of any kind of tyranny." In his *Cours de politique constitutionelle* (1816) he wrote: "For forty years I have fought for the same principle: liberty in all things, in religion, in philosophy, in literature, in industry, in politics. By liberty I mean the triumph of the individual as much over the government that seeks to rule by despotic methods as over the masses who try to enslave minorities. Despotism has no rights at all. A majority has the right to force the minority to respect public order. But anything which does not affect public order, anything which by its expression does no harm to anyone else (whether by inciting to a breach of the peace or by suppressing contrary opinions), anything which in industry does not limit free competition—all these things pertain to the individual and not to the state. As such, they cannot be subjected to the power of the state."

Constant understood that the decisive question was not so much whether the king or the people, a legislative assembly or an emperor, was the sovereign, but whether any limits, and which limits, were set to the exercise of sovereignty. The guardians of such limited power were the freedoms of press and public opinion and the publicity of finance. Its presupposition was the abandonment of French militarism and hegemonial aspirations. The régime of Louis Philippe and his Prime Minister, François Guizot (1787-1874), a French Protestant and historian who studied the English revolutions, seemed to realize these presuppositions. But its spirit of peace and compromise was such an anti-climax to the great and heroic times of the Revolution and of Napoleon, that France felt bored. Even greater harm was done by the fact that the French propertied classes, now in power, did not realize the need for the adaptation of the social system to a rapidly changing economic order. The English propertied classes, after 1830, learned the necessity for timely and sustained concessions and thereby established a developing social peace. The French liberal tradition suffered from the beginning from an insufficient sense of social responsibility. The philanthropic initiative and the moral self-restraint, which were not unknown among the English bourgeoisie, were far more seldom found in France.

Anglophobia and Germanomania. After 1815 the growth of a tradition of liberty was hampered by the widespread feeling of enmity to England. The close cultural contact between the two countries which had existed in the eighteenth century was replaced by a Germanomania which swept intellectual France after 1815. The Revolution and Napoleon had found themselves thwarted by England in their triumphal march to European hegemony. The French forgot the defeat at Leipzig and the victories of the Prussian Field-Marshal Blücher. They remembered Waterloo and Wellington as symbols of the imperial humiliation. Britain, whose own conquest of liberty had engendered the growth of liberty in France, appeared overpowering and insolent; Germany, where many thinkers rejected the ideas of the French Revolution and of liberty, seemed peaceful and idyllic. She was little known except through the eyes of Madame de Staël (1766-1817). In her book *De l'Allemagne* (1812) she drew a heart-warming picture of a people of poets and thinkers who led a modest and virtuous existence in small picturesque towns without ambitions for power. Madame de Staël, who hardly knew German, was unaware of the forward-driving forces which were transforming Germany in her own day. She wished to confront France with the example of a virtuous though largely imaginary country, and to oppose the

inspiration of German poetic enthusiasm to the coldness
of the Napoleonic empire. German romanticism aroused
her ardent sympathies which she communicated to the
young generations in France. French scholars began to
go to Germany to study. Victor Cousin (1792-1867)
popularized German philosophy before enthusiastic audiences at the Sorbonne.

Panaceas: Proposal for a "Leader."   Imperialists
and republicans alike kept the faith in France's mission
alive. They maintained that, threatened by East and
West, France could not afford the luxury of a liberal
development with the accompanying divisions of interests,
parties, and classes. France needed national unity above
all. Writing in 1839, Louis Napoleon saw "at the present
day only two governments which can fulfill their provi-
dential mission. These are the two colossi, which exist,
one at the extremity of the New, the other at the extremity of the Old World. Whilst our European center
resembles a volcano which consumes itself in its crater,
the two nations of the East and the West march without
hesitation on the road of improvement, one of them
through the will of one man, the other through liberty."
The way of the East: Russian autocracy; the way of the
West: American and English liberty; which path was
France to follow? The future Napoleon III suggested a
third road for France: a strong, unified government, "the
beneficent motive power of all social organization," supported by the people. France could not fulfill her mission
if she exhausted her energies in "never-ending internal
contests." Louis Napoleon offered himself as the man
to lead a strong, unified France. Almost a century later
the *Enciclopedia Italiana* in its article on the doctrine of
Fascism defined Fascism as "the purest form of democracy, if the nation is conceived, as it should be, quali-
tatively and not quantitatively, as the most powerful,
most moral, most coherent, truest idea, which acts within
the nation as the conscience and will of a few, even of
One. It is an ideal which tends to become active within
the conscience and the will of all, that is to say, of all
those who rightly constitute a nation and have set out
upon the same line of development and spiritual formation as one conscience and a sole will."

The People as Bearers of France's Mission. This one conscience and sole will of the nation could be embodied in the Emperor. Others looked to the People as its mystical embodiment and as the bearer of France's mission. According to the French historian Jules Michelet (1798-1874) the People, through the Revolution, became the incarnation of France. Michelet dedicated his life to writing the history of his nation. He saw the Revolution as its climax, and the celebration on July 14, 1790, as the climax of the Revolution. On that day the French masses spontaneously proclaimed their joyful union, a union which excluded none. "At no other time," Michelet believed, "has man's heart been wiser or more spacious, at no other time have distinctions of class, of fortune, and of party been more completely forgotten." On July 14, 1790, Michelet insisted, and not under the Terror or under Napoleon, France had been truly united, ready for the fulfillment of her mission, in which Michelet believed as firmly as Robespierre and Bonaparte. (*See Reading No. 12.*)

Michelet shared the general enthusiasm for Germany. His friend Edgar Quinet (1803-1875) expressed their common feelings, when as a young man, in the preface to his translation of Herder, he paid tribute to Germany, "the land of the soul and of hope, where under the oaks of Arminius, the pure spring of moral duty gushes forth and where sooner or later the neighboring peoples will come to quench their thirst." Compared with German poetry and philosophy, England appeared materialistic; whereas France led the movement of the modern spirit, England was regarded as the land of the *status quo.* France represented heroism, martial virtues, and progress; England was a commercialized nation, eager for peace and profit. The peaceful policy of France under Louis Philippe seemed to Michelet a betrayal of France's national mission: bourgeois interests and national grandeur seemed to exclude each other. Like Louis Napoleon, Michelet saw France between East and West, threatened by both, finding her salvation only in integral unity. "Who has an army? We alone do," Michelet wrote in his *Le Peuple.* "England and Russia, two weak and bloated giants, deceive Europe. They are great empires but weak peoples. Let France be One, for one moment. She will be as strong as the whole world." Michelet disparaged "the perpetual peace which some promise you, while the arsenals (of Russia and England) smoke. Let us try peace by beginning to cement it among ourselves. One people! One fatherland! One France!" Michelet accused the French bourgeoisie of lacking the sentiment of military honor and of being subservient to British interests and ideas. He had confidence only in the people of France, ever-renewed "by our heroic legend, the invisible spirit of the heroes of our wars, the wind of the old flag." Turning to the people, Michelet exclaimed: "If the world can be saved by war, you alone can save it. Sacred bayonets of France, take care that nothing darkens that light which shines over you and which no eye can bear." Michelet wrote these lines in 1846, at a time when the messianic expectations of the French Revolution were fanned again.

Tocqueville as Prophet of Liberty.   In the gales of the aroused heroic passions and social unrest at the beginning of 1848, the complacent liberal tradition of the bourgeois monarchy demonstrated its fragility. One of the few liberals who foresaw the coming storm was Alexis Comte de Tocqueville (1805-1859), a descendant of the old French Catholic nobility. He was convinced of the inevitability of the advent of democracy in the world's affairs. He went to the United States to study the workings of democracy there. He too acknowledged himself a passionate lover of liberty. He wished to see it developed in all the institutions of France. "But at the same time," he wrote in a letter in 1836, "I shall profess so great a respect for justice, so true a love for order and law, so deep and reasonable an attachment for morality and religious beliefs, that I cannot but believe that people will plainly see in me a liberal of a new kind and will not confuse me with the majority of the democrats of today." Hopefully he pointed to the United States. There democracy, in power then for more than sixty years, had created not only the most prosperous but the most stable of all the nations. With almost all of Europe, with the exception of England, convulsed by revolutions, America remained at peace. For there,

Tocqueville wrote, "the republic has not been the assailant but the guardian of all vested rights. The property of individuals had had better guarantees there than in any other country. Anarchy has been as unknown there as despotism." Tocqueville learned from England and America the importance of the free organization of individuals in powerful associations, to safeguard their economic, social or cultural interests against the state and even against the pressure of majorities. "Through association private citizens can form very wealthy, powerful and influential bodies. An association, whether political, industrial, commercial, scientific or literary, is itself an enlightened and powerful citizen who cannot be brought to heel at the whim of authority or secretly oppressed. Constitutional government can produce its best result only through the struggle of collective interests, organized and pleading their own case." (*See Readings Nos. 13, 14.*)

Tortuous Road of the Liberal Tradition. In his last book *L'Ancien Régime et la Révolution* (1856) Tocqueville no longer saw the French Revolution as a new beginning, as a complete break with the preceding absolutist régime, but as its continuation and result. He was afraid lest the new revolutionary age should lead to a new arbitrary despotism either of a faction or of an individual. He understood the dangers to which the principle of equality exposed the independence of man, but he did not think that they were insurmountable. He trusted in the growing sense of individual liberty and the freedom of association, but he knew that these attitudes demand a long habit. The events of 1848 showed how little these habits were yet rooted in France. February 1848 ushered in a brief era of enthusiastic hopes and mirages, but only four months later, in June, the social unrest led to a bitter civil war. The spectre of the red terror, of the revolutionary Parisian masses, frightened the bourgeoisie and the peasantry. The workers felt themselves victims of a white terror. Finally, less than ten months after the proclamation of the republic, none other but Louis Napoleon was elected as its first President by an immense majority of the people. Four years later even the nominal existence of the Second Republic came to an end. The Second Empire was born with the acclaim of the masses.

The masses had supported Napoleon I. The invading enemy armies, not the people, had put an end to his régime in 1814. When he returned from Elba the following year, the Emperor encountered practically no resistance in France. The people welcomed him. Four decades later, the French people welcomed Napoleon III. He promised glory and prosperity: these meant more to the people than individual liberty. He confidently introduced general suffrage. He knew that opposition to his régime would come rather from the educated and propertied classes than from the masses. Yet the Second Empire turned out to be the period in which a free public opinion grew in influence, and the liberal tradition began to take root. After the fall of the Empire, France established a republican régime, moderate and liberal, which in spite of its shortcomings endured. The provisional Constitution of 1875 remained in power for many decades. The time of successive revolutions and counter-revolutions belonged to the past. Yet in France the liberal tradition was never as generally accepted by the entire people as in England or the United States. Again and again it was attacked from the right or left, by absolutist traditionalism or by utopian radicalism. Yet so far, France has always emerged victorious from these trials. In 1940 the Third Republic seemed buried under the onslaught of the traditionalist Right, supported by outside forces. At that time the ruling clique in France once more turned against England, with her liberalism and commercialism. But when, through the fortunes of war, the traditionalist régime became a brief interlude, and the Fourth Republic emerged, the strength of the liberal tradition in France asserted itself. The Fourth Republic was a continuation of the Third Republic, in closer unity with Britain and the West than France had ever been.

Rôle of Clericalism. The Second Empire was the seedtime of the liberal tradition in France. It made men like Michelet more critical of the people in general. The French people no longer appeared as the model of democratic virtues. The closer alliance between Napoleon

III and the Catholic church demonstrated the dangers of clericalism. In his younger years, Michelet had appreciated the glories of the French Catholic Middle Ages. Later, he still clung to Christianity as the highest ideal. The French Revolution then appeared to him as the fulfillment of pure Christianity against the corruption of the church, as the supreme expression of the spirit of the gospel. Now he interpreted the Revolution as the rejection of Christianity and all that it implied. Moreover, Michelet himself grew less radical and less absolutist in his revolutionary faith. He now understood that the enduring achievements in history were settlements through adjustment and reconciliation, in the spirit of tolerance. He worked for "a union with the slow fusion of differences, assimilation by tactful consideration, a careful respect for mutual liberty." Michelet reproached the people for being subject to idolatry, an inclination which made the reign of men like Robespierre or Napoleon possible. "Idolatry is no longer permissible," he wrote. "Away with prejudices! Away with sanguinary systems, away with historical fetishes, Caesar or Robespierre! Away with the deification of the people!"

The Example of Britain. The Revolution of 1848 failed in France as it failed in Germany. In the former, it opened the way for Napoleon III; in the latter, for Bismarck. But the number of leading German intellectuals who openly opposed Bismarck was small. The strength of the growing liberal tradition in France was shown by the number of intellectuals who went into silence or exile. The opposition in France forced Napoleon III to make concessions. With the growth of liberalism, France turned to England again. In 1847 Michelet had written that "France and Germany, suffocated between two giants, of whom one rules the sea and the other the land, have no better security for the future than their union." England appeared to him as "*l'anti-France.*" "The war of all wars, the struggle of all struggles is that between Britain and France," he wrote. "The rest are episodes." The Glorious Revolution seemed insignificant compared to the French Revolution. To many Frenchmen of the period Britain appeared as a rich country but one without soul or ideas, as did

America a century later. But the experience of the Second Empire made even Michelet change his point of view. The Glorious Revolution, so prosaic in its appearances, had led to a steady and uninterrupted growth of liberty. The French Revolutions of 1789 and 1848, with their dramatic enthusiasm, had ushered in the Napoleonic Empires. Completing his *History of France*, Michelet viewed the nineteenth century as a struggle between British capitalism and Napoleonic militarism. He still thoroughly disliked industrialism and commercialism, yet he now believed them to be the lesser evil compared to Napoleon. He declared himself for Britain, against Louis XIV and Napoleon; for constitutional liberty, against military grandeur. "The Channel already seemed bridged by common ideas and even by common interests," he wrote in his last year. "I am happy to learn of the project of a tunnel from Calais to Dover which would restore the two countries to their real neighborliness, their kinship, their geological identity."

The German Danger. While the bonds with England were being strengthened, some tenacious illusions about Germany were dispelled. Since 1831, Quinet had tried unsuccessfully to draw France's attention to the growing influence of Prussia's "popular despotism" over the leading German minds. He saw veneration for the Prussian Sword and authority spreading throughout Germany. One of the first to recognize this rising danger, he warned that France could not meet it by mere militarism. Only a France alive to the traditions of liberty could counter an authoritarian and nationalistic Germany. An openly avowed militarism, Quinet insisted, was less dangerous than one which assumed the mask of liberty, for in the latter case all notions of true and false became hopelessly confounded and harm was done to the very soul of the people. Bismarck, at least, did not claim to be a champion of democracy and popular sovereignty. Napoleon III had assumed this pose, and this had gained for him the support of the masses. "There is nothing older in the world," Quinet wrote, "than people who acclaim success, who welcome in the evening what they cursed in the morning. It is useless to create a new word for that, 'authoritarian democracy,' as if any authority placed in the stead of law were not the very negation of democracy. Is that the way to form great nations? I have so often seen democracy and liberty taken in by cheap promises of establishing freedom sometime in the future, after strength and union have done their work. But meanwhile the masses have become impenetrable to the ideas of justice and liberty."

The New Faith of Ernest Renan. The Franco-Prussian war of 1870 destroyed the dominating fascination of the Napoleonic legend and the illusions about Germany's nature. Among those who were deeply shocked by the revelations of the war was Ernest Renan (1823-1892), the leading French scholar and humanist of the period. He had been an ardent admirer of German culture and science and always acknowledged a deep indebtedness to them. His disillusionment did not turn him into a French nationalist. It set him thinking about the meaning of nationalism, the future of liberty in France and of peace and civilization in Europe. (*See Readings Nos. 15, 16, 17.*) "I had always dreamt," he wrote after the war, "of working for the intellectual, moral and political alliance with Germany. Such an alliance would also win the adherence of Britain. Together the three could constitute a force capable of directing the world toward a liberal civilization, equally remote from the naively blind haste of democracy and the childish whims of a return to the past." Renan continued to hope for a league of free men of good will from all nations, who would create and maintain, above the bitter national struggles, a firmament of pure ideas, where there would be neither Greek nor barbarian, neither German nor Latin.

In his life and personality Renan reflected many of the great currents of the period. By environmental and family traditions he was "born to be a priest." At the age of twenty he entered the famous seminary of St. Sulpice in Paris, but two years later he regretfully abandoned the preparation for priesthood. "Catholicism, like a fairy circle," he wrote, "casts such a powerful spell upon one's whole life, that when one is deprived of it, everything seems aimless and gloomy. The whole universe appeared to me an arid and chilly desert. With

Christianity untrue, everything seemed indifferent, frivolous, and undeserving of interest." Having abandoned the priesthood of the church, Renan devoted himself with equal earnestness and moral integrity to the secular priesthood of learning. For a short time he developed, together with his fellow student Marcelin Berthelot (1827-1907), the future famous chemist, a religion of science. In 1848 he summed up this new faith in a long and laborious book, *L'Avenir de la Science*. "By every way open to us we begin to proclaim the right of human reason to reform society by means of rational science. We can state without exaggeration that science holds the future of humanity. Science alone can explain human destiny and teach the way of attaining it. The scientific organization of mankind is the final word of modern science, its bold but legitimate pretension."

Renan did not publish his youthful book until forty years later. His fundamental conviction remained the same. "My religion now as ever is the progress of reason, in other words, the progress of science." But the experience of forty years had made him more cautious. He no longer shared Condorcet's faith in the omnipotence of science nor Comte's confidence in the omniscience of scientists. "The main error with which these old pages teem is an exaggerated optimism which is determined not to see the continuous existence of evil. The reader will also notice an old leaven of Catholicism, the idea that we shall see the age of faith once more when a compulsory and universal religion will prevail as it did in the Middle Ages. Heaven preserve us from being saved in that fashion!" Like so many others, Renan realized that the progress of science had not been matched by a similar advance in man's moral and spiritual life. But he did not look for the remedy in an old or new orthodoxy. A catechism, whether theological or positivist, would be much too dearly bought by a return to the credulity and the fanaticism of the Middle Ages. Certainly, science could not reveal the whole truth, but it could protect men against error. Looking back on almost half a century of a life devoted to scholarship, Renan did not hesitate to reaffirm his faith in science.

The Future of Liberty in France. But what was

the future of liberty in a France demoralized by the Empire, shaken in its confidence by military defeat and the civil war of the Commune? Was France not, as the Germans claimed, decadent and played out? Was she able to establish a régime which would endure, equidistant from ever-renewed revolutionary anarchy and from the dead hand of despotism and clericalism? Edouard de Laboulaye (1819-1893), in his *Le Parti Liberal* (1871), expressed these doubts about the future of liberty in France: "When has France had her freedom? When have we not been 'protected' by officials? When has it been possible without special permission for churches to open, for masters to teach, for citizens to meet or join? When has the press been entirely free? When have provinces or communes really been mistresses of their rights?" Even the Third Republic did not establish these freedoms as they are known in England or the United States. Was there not ground for pessimism? Hippolyte Taine (1828-1893), who was, along with Renan, the greatest influence on the younger generation of his time, devoted his last years to the search for the origins of modern France. As a disciple of Comte he rejected metaphysics and abstract principles. Was not the weakness of France due to the fact that the *ancien régime* as well as the Revolution was dominated by abstract and absolutist ideas? Royalty, Revolution, and Empire equally suppressed the intermediary autonomous association between the central authority and the individual. This created "boredom, egoism, indifference to public affairs, the stultification of many life-forces, the narrowness of provincial life." Taine knew that the *ancien régime* had to be reformed. "The old machine had rusted and was fit only to be thrown away." Such an operation could, however, be effected in two different ways; the way of Locke, which England followed, or the way of Rousseau, which France followed. Taine detested the latter way. The French Revolution was to him "the revolt of asses and horses against men," but he immediately pointed out that for the two preceding centuries "men had been treated as asses and horses." The monarchy under Louis XIV had destroyed personal initiative and freedom of association and thus prepared the Revolution and the Empire.

Taine believed even more strongly in reason and science than did Renan in his later years. But science was no longer the great revolutionary force that had inspired Condorcet and the young Renan. "It appears to me," Taine wrote to Guizot in 1873, "that general science tends towards prudence and conservatism, not toward revolution, and for proof of this we need but to study the delicate complexity of the social body. This will easily defend us from all charlatanism and general panaceas, radical or simple." The picture which emerged from Taine's great historical work was thoroughly pessimistic. Not without justification the historian Gabriel Monod (1844-1912) wrote him in 1878: "According to you the *ancien régime,* the Revolution, the Empire, were all fiascos, which explain why we are now marking time in the mud. Granted you are right, but if it is all as bad as that, how is it that we are still alive?" And France was very much alive in 1878.

Acceptance and Defense of the Liberal Régime. The Republic and the liberal tradition were slowly but surely accepted. The development in France was entirely different from that which took place under similar circumstances in Germany half a century later. In 1919 Germany faced a situation comparable to that of France in 1871. The imperial army had been defeated; the imperial régime was replaced by a republic reluctantly accepted; revolts of the working classes threatened the social order. In both cases the republic elected former imperial marshals as presidents, in the case of France, Marshal MacMahon (1808-1893); in the case of Germany, Paul von Hindenburg. MacMahon was forced to resign by the triumphant republic; Hindenburg helped to bury the republic in the triumph of Hitlerism. The liberal régime in France, even after its installation in 1875, has never been secure. Yet, whenever it was threatened, the majority of the people rallied to its defense.

THE CATHOLIC TRADITION

Catholic France. The liberal tradition in France looked to the West. From there its original inspiration had come. Victor Duc de Broglie (1785-1870), the son-in-law of Madame de Staël and for some time Minister of Foreign Affairs and Prime Minister under Louis Philippe, wrote in his *Souvenirs* which were published after his death: "Without despising or deprecating the *ancien régime,* I believe any attempt to restore it futile. Both by heart and by conviction, I belong to the new society. I sincerely believe in its indefinite progress, and while hating the revolutionary spirit and the disorder it entails, I look upon the United States of America as representing the future of civilized countries and upon the English monarchy as the government of today. Hating despotism, I saw in limited monarchy a transitional stage." But Catholic, Jacobin, Napoleonic France did not look to the West; their inspiration came from Rome. The Jacobins found their model in the Roman Republic and in Brutus; Napoleon was inspired by the glory of the Roman Empire and Caesar; Catholic France looked to the See of St. Peter in Rome.

None of these traditions was more deeply rooted in French history than the Catholic tradition. France was "the oldest daughter of the church," and the French monarch, "the most Christian king." Though a part of the universal Catholic church, the French church, nevertheless, possessed a distinctively national character. It supported the independence of France against the secular jurisdiction of the Pope. In 1682 the Gallican Declaration, drawn up by Bishop Bossuet (1627-1704), the most renowned prelate of the realm, asserted "that kings and sovereigns are not, by God's command, subject to any ecclesiastical power in temporal matters. They cannot be deposed, directly or indirectly, by the authority of the heads of the church. Their subjects cannot be dispensed from obedience." And in another passage the Declaration emphasized that "although the Pope has chief voice in questions of faith, still his decision is not unalterable unless the consent of the church is given." This self-assertion of the French church under the monarchy is unknown to modern French Catholicism. The French Revolution dealt the church's hitherto all-dominant position such a blow that from then on it leaned more and more upon Rome. De Maistre, himself not a citizen of France but a subject of the king of Sardinia, pointed the way in his glorification of the Pope's temporal power as the surest safeguard against the Revolution.

Rome Beyond the Mountains. From the Revolution on, the church no longer represented the entire nation but became a participant in the civil wars and conflicts which rent France asunder. The church—and this means in Catholic countries Christianity itself—became a political issue and often the most burning one. The church in France after the Revolution aligned itself predominantly with the forces of the *ancien régime* against the spirit of 1789 and against liberalism. At the same time the Papal Curia successfully tightened its organizational and spiritual hold over the entire Catholic church, to a degree hardly foreseen in the eighteenth century. Then the Catholic monarchs of France, Austria, Spain, and Portugal had successfully fought off any interference from the Roman see in political or social questions. Upon their demands, Pope Clement XIV in 1773 had even suppressed the Jesuit Order, which was the chief instrument of papal influence in the Catholic nations. Immediately after the end of the Revolution, in 1814, Pope Pius VII restored the order. A new emphasis was put on the obedience of Catholics everywhere to the Holy See. They were told to look to Rome beyond the mountains, *ultra montes,* for guidance not only in spiritual but also in political matters. The Gallican trend in the French church receded before the growing Ultramontane trend.

Pius IX's War on Modernism. Two great popes, whose reigns represented the two longest pontificates in the history of the papacy and who together occupied the papal throne for fifty-five years, Pius IX (1792-1878) and Leo XIII (1810-1903), committed the papacy to the principles of Ultramontanism. Pius IX ascended the throne in 1846. For two years he sympathized mildly with liberal reforms and Italian nationalism. The experience of the Revolution of 1848, with the creation of the short-lived Roman Republic in the Papal State, changed his outlook. The national unification of Italy went even further in alienating the Pope's sympathies for modern movements. As a consequence of the process of unification, the Papal State, which had lasted for over 1000 years, was abolished, and the separation of state and church was introduced not only throughout Italy but in Rome itself. From 1849 on, Pius IX warred determinedly against the influence of modernism on every aspect of life. He strengthened the Catholic faith by an emphasis on liturgic revival and on the adoration of the Virgin. In 1858, a young girl, Bernadette (1844-1878), had a vision of the apparition of Mary in Lourdes. The Bull *Ineffabilis Deus* proclaimed the Dogma of the Immaculate Conception. Prosper Guéranger (1805-1875) made the Benedictine Abbey of Solesmes the center of the resurgence of an aesthetic Catholicism which was greatly in the manner of Chateaubriand's glorification of the beauty of religion.

"Syllabus of the Principal Errors of Our Time." The papal efforts of opposition to modern civilization culminated in the *"Syllabus of the Principal Errors of Our Time."* It was published in December 1864, together with the Encyclical *Quanta Cura,* and contained the most important authoritarian and dogmatic challenge to modern civilization, issued by the most ancient and venerable institution of Christendom. The Syllabus condemned eighty errors as incompatible with the Catholic faith. Among them were the following: That the church ought to tolerate the errors of philosophy, leaving to philosophy the care of their corrections; that every man is free to embrace and profess a religion which he, guided by the light of reason, believes to be true; that the eternal salvation may (at least) be hoped for by all those who are not within the true church of Christ; that Protestantism is another form of the same true Christian religion, in which it is as possible to please God as in the Catholic faith; that in a conflict between ecclesiastical and civil law, civil law takes precedence; that there should be separation of church and state; that today the Catholic religion can no longer be regarded as the only religion of state, to the exclusion of all other cults; that the Roman Pontiff can, and ought to, reconcile himself to, and agree with, progress, liberalism, modern civilization.

Church Claims to Universal Authority. This claim to the control of all cultural and intellectual life by the church was not new, yet its uncompromising reassertion in the nineteenth century was startling. It deepened the irreconcilable conflict between the church and modern civilization, but at the same time it strengthened the church and the position of the Pope. In 1869 Pius IX called the first Ecumenical Council of the Catholic Church since the Council of Trent in the sixteenth Century. The Council met in the Vatican, and on July 18, 1870, it defined, in a solemn decree, the primacy and infallibility of the Pope. By an irony of history, two months later, the Papal State ceased to exist. In a plebiscite the population voted overwhelmingly for the unification of the Papal State with the Kingdom of Italy. The Pope rejected this spoliation of the See of Saint Peter; yet the loss of his position as one of the princes of Italy and his ensuing non-involvement in the wars and policies of the peninsula probably strengthened the universal authority of the papacy.

France and the Papal State. From 1849 to 1870, the independence of the Papal State had been maintained exclusively with the help of French armed forces, which the régime of Louis Napoleon put at the disposal of the church. French troops were instrumental in defeating the Roman Republic of Giuseppe Mazzini and Giuseppe Garibaldi. Under French protection, the Pope returned to Rome after the Revolution of 1848. When the Catholic empire of Napoleon III was defeated by Protestant Prussia at Sedan in the beginning of September 1870, the French troops were withdrawn from Rome. Their withdrawal brought about the end of the Papal State. Thus the histories of France and of the Catholic church

were intellectually and politically interwoven in the
nineteenth century.

Struggle for Control of Education. The historical
struggle between modern civilization and the Catholic
church manifested itself within France primarily in the
controversy over the control of education. Under the
ancien régime the church, especially the Jesuits, enjoyed
an educational monopoly. The Revolution theoretically
and Napoleon practically replaced this monopoly with a
monopoly of the state. The secular state proclaimed by
the Revolution was only theoretically neutral in matters
of religion; in practice it was often as combative as the
church itself. Under the Restoration and bourgeois monarchies compromise solutions were reached, and much
of the secondary education, especially that of young
women, returned to ecclesiastical hands. Ironically, only
under Louis Napoleon, who had started his life as a free-
thinking Carbonaro and a revolutionary nationalist in
Italy, did the church achieve its educational goal. As
head of the French state, Louis Napoleon became more
subservient to the church than the Catholic monarchs
had been. The *Loi Falloux* of March 15, 1850—so
named after Comte Frédéric Falloux (1811-1886) who
was then Minister of Education—reorganized elementary
and secondary education, putting elementary schools under the management of the local curates and giving to
the Catholic clergy and members of religious orders the
right to teach without certification or qualification by
the state. The influence of the church was so great that
in 1863 Renan was removed from his chair at the Collège
de France for publishing *La Vie de Jésus,* in which he
treated the founder of the Christian religion as merely
a human though exalted being. Gratefully Louis Veuillot
(1818-1883), the leader of the Ultramontane faction
among the French Catholics, acknowledged in 1854 that
no other man could have done for religion and social
order what Louis Napoleon had done. "Under him the
church enjoys a freedom she has not had for centuries.
She may have been stronger under the old monarchy,
but she was less free." The large majority of French
Catholics followed Louis Veuillot and supported Napoleon III.

Liberal Catholicism. Yet there was a small group of prominent and devout French Catholics, who like other liberal French intellectuals rejected the despotism of Napoleon III and remained faithful to the liberal tradition of modern civilization. Their leaders were Jean Baptiste Henri Lacordaire (1802-1861) and Comte Charles de Montalembert (1810-1870). Both were originally under the influence of Lamennais but separated from him when he left the church. In their religious views they were orthodox and unquestioningly accepted the authority of the Pope. In their political views they demanded the freedoms of education, of association, and of the press. They were convinced that in Western Europe, in Britain and France, in Germany and Italy, the modern state had come to stay. In those states the Catholics were either in the minority or, if they formed a majority, they were unable to enforce conformity to the Catholic tradition upon the state or the entire people. Under these conditions liberty safeguarded the rights and position of the Catholic church in modern society. The liberal Catholics in France wished to conciliate the aspirations of the modern age with the doctrines of the Gospel. Living in a society in which secularism grew rapidly, they wished to attract the indifferent and often hostile crowd, especially the youth. They wanted, as Montalembert said, to throw a new light upon the immutable eternal truths by adapting them to the needs and habits of modern minds.

In an address to the Catholic Congress in Malines on August 21, 1863, Montalembert spoke on "A Free Church in a Free State." He distinguished between dogmatic intolerance, which was inseparable from the eternal truth, and civic tolerance which was indispensable to the modern state. "Not against the church, but against the state, and only against the state, I vindicate that freedom of conscience which is at once man's right, merit, and supreme danger. But we have to recognize that the enthusiastic devotion to religious liberty which animates me is not widely accepted among Catholics. They would like such liberty for themselves, but there is no great merit in this; everyone desires all kinds of liberties for himself." Montalembert pointed out that the experience of the nineteenth century had proven that Catholicism and the Christian faith flourished in free societies, whereas in Italy, Spain, and Portugal, the system of enforced religion, the old alliance of altar and throne, had been proven incapable of defending Catholicism or of preventing the penetration of revolutionary ideas. In fact, Montalembert could point out, anticlericalism and an anti-religious spirit were nowhere stronger than in countries with a Catholic religion of state. "Under the superficial crust of the union of church and state, or even of the subordination of state to church, the revolutionary lava had hollowed out its bed and silently consumed the souls which had become its prey. At the first blow, everything crumbled. These paradises of religious absolutism have become the scandal and despair of all Catholic hearts. Everywhere today, as in the first centuries of the church, Catholicism descends into the arena, struggles and resists, endures and triumphs in the name of freedom of conscience." Explaining his concept of a free church in a free state Montalembert stressed that "a free state does not mean a government which can do as it pleases. On the contrary, a state is the freer the more its government is limited. No one will dare to say that Russia is a free state, precisely because the ruler there disposes freely of the lives, the goods and the honor of his unfortunate subjects. Everyone, on the other hand, recognizes that England is a free state, precisely because its government is more limited than any other." The demand for a free church in a free state distinguished the liberal Catholics from the intolerant Catholics who reject the free state, and from those inconsistent liberals who reject the free church. (*See Reading No. 19.*)

Rejection of the Liberal Tradition. The liberal Catholics remained a minority in France. To their left were the liberals and radicals who decried the church and its dogma. To their right was the majority of the Catholics and of the hierarchy, supported by Pius IX, who denied the possibility or desirability of a compromise with liberalism and modern society. Their most prominent spokesman was Louis Veuillot who in 1842 became the editor-in-chief of the Catholic organ *l'Uni-*

vers. In his first editorial he wrote: "In the midst of factions of every sort, we belong only to the church and to our country. With justice towards all, submissive to the laws of the church, we reserve our homage and our love for an authority of genuine worth, an authority which will issue from the present anarchy and will demonstrably stem from God, marching towards the new destinies of France, with Cross in hands." At the end of 1855 Veuillot wrote: "The church gives you all the freedom that decent people want and which is essential to human dignity."

Veuillot was the foremost disciple of de Maistre in modern France. He rejected the entire liberal tradition. For him, France was identical with Catholic France: Protestants and others did not belong. He never accepted the republic after 1870. It appeared to him not only unChristian but unFrench. "I, a Catholic Christian of France, as old in France as its oaks and venerable as they; I, son of a race which has never ceased giving to France tillers of the soil, soldiers and priests, and who asks nothing in return but work, the Eucharist, and rest in the shadow of the Cross; . . . I am made, unmade, governed, ruled, slashed at by vagabonds of mind and morals, men who are neither Christians nor Catholics, and by that very fact, who are not French and who can have no love of France." (*See Reading No. 20.*) Veuillot rejected any peace or compromise with the France which originated in 1789.

Ultramontanism versus the French Republic. When the French Republic was firmly established in 1875, Ultramontane Catholicism understandably assumed a hostile position. The republican leader, Léon Gambetta (1838-1882), exclaimed in a speech on May 4, 1877, *"Le clericalisme, voilà l'ennemi!"* ("Clericalism is our enemy.") The republican and liberal feeling among the French people was so strong that this battle cry brought victory in the elections of 1877 to the republican and anti-clerical forces. The legislation which followed freed education from church control imposed by the *Loi Falloux* and restored divorce. But the struggle between liberalism and Catholicism was by no means over. In the two great crises which the Republican régime underwent in the following two decades, the Boulanger agitation and the Dreyfus Affair, most Catholics were found in the anti-republican camp.

Only the diplomatic skill of Pope Leo XIII brought about a rapprochement of the Catholics with the Republic: *le ralliement*. By his statesmanship and his great interest in scholarship and literature, Leo XIII raised the prestige of the papacy to a height unknown in modern times. He reformed the teaching in Catholic academies and universities and made the renewed study of Thomas Aquinas its foundation. And now of all the Catholic countries, it was France, with her religious and intellectual freedom assured by the Third Republic, which produced the leading scholars and writers of the neo-Catholic school.

Attempts to Revive Liberal Catholicism. Of equal importance for French Catholicism was the encyclical letter *Rerum Novarum* in which Leo XIII turned his attention to the condition of the working class. The Catholic church has always opposed economic individualism and capitalism. With the inroads of "atheistic" socialism among the industrial workers, particularly in Catholic countries such as France, Belgium, the Rhineland, Silesia, Italy, and Austria, the Pope in his encyclical letter appealed to the Catholic workingman and recalled Catholic capitalists and governments to the principles of the church. Forty years later, on May 15, 1931, in the Encyclical *Quadragesimo Anno,* Pope Pius XI reiterated and elaborated the admonition of his predecessor against economic liberalism and for social legislation. In this more moderate atmosphere attempts were made in France to revive liberal Catholicism and to fill it with social implications. In 1897 Marc Sangnier started the movement called *Sillon* (Furrow) which, however, was condemned by Pope Pius X in 1910. The following year a new movement, *Jeune République,* tried to reconcile the Catholic faith and republican democracy. In Italy, which faced problems similar to those of France, a Catholic priest, Luigi Sturzo, founded the *Partito Populare Italiano* in 1919. In 1924 this party favored a coalition with the Socialists in opposition to Fascism, a program, however, which the church, outstandingly the

Jesuits, rejected. But the defeat of Fascism in Italy and France in World War II by the Western democracies changed the situation and made the church more inclined to tolerate a reconciliation between modern democracy and the Catholic church. Such was the program of the *Mouvement Républicain Populaire* in France, which in the first years after the downfall of the clerical-conservative regime of Marshal Pétain, rallied a large number of Catholics to the support of democracy.

The Urge to Compromise. In the twentieth century, on the whole, the controversy over the position of the Catholic church in the modern French state lost much of its bitterness. There was a greater readiness on both sides to accept a compromise solution based upon the recognition of the freedoms which the French people had gained in 1789. This readiness was increased, on the one hand, by the decisive victory which the liberal forces achieved in the Dreyfus Affair, by the triumph of the Republic in World War I, and by its alliance with the Western democracies. The new attitude was aided, on the other hand, by the growing ascendancy of the Catholic tradition over many French intellectuals and writers, a literary renascence which, as Montalembert had foreseen, was made possible by the very atmosphere of freedom which the Third Republic had created.

— 6 —

LITERATURE AND SOCIETY

Complexity of French Literary Development. Writers and artists, not generals and statesmen, created the enduring glory of modern France. The baffling complex-

ity of their contributions offers the most representative
picture of the trends of continental intellectual life since
the Revolution. The liberal tradition assured an unprecedented freedom of arts and letters in France. Yet the
same period witnessed a strange but characteristic development: many of France's great writers and intellectuals found themselves in bitter opposition to modern
liberal society. They frequently felt outside the society,
suffering from its conventions, opposed to its standards,
and thwarted by its indifference. Modern middle-class
society, which rose to power in France in 1830 and definitively established itself with the Third Republic, appeared to them the embodiment of drab mediocrity. They
turned away from it to nostalgic dreams of the past, to
a quest for heroic grandeur, to apocalyptic expectations
of a brilliant future, or they resigned themselves to a
feeling of indifference or despair. From the Romanticists
after the Napoleonic Wars to the Surrealists after the
First World War, many French artists lived, actually or
ideologically, outside society, representing movements of
protest or revolt.

**The Literary Artist and the Explosive Social Struc-
ture.** The Romanticists suffered from the then *mal du
siècle* (the malady of the century) which Alfred de
Musset (1810-1857) described in his autobiographical
novel *La Confession d'un Enfant du Siècle* (1835). The
rapid changes ushered in by the Revolution and Napoleon had destroyed the traditional social structure of
France and left all minds bewildered. All established
values had become doubtful. Everything seemed to be in
transition, and this insecurity was interpreted by many
as a decline. A century later, the generation emerging
from the First World War faced a similar collapse of a
social order and of a system of values. Both catastrophes
left in their aftermath a climate of melancholy exhaustion and great expectations. The present seemed unbearable. The way out seemed to lead either to a glorified
past or to a utopian future. "A feeling of extreme uneasi-
ness began to ferment in all young hearts," Musset wrote
about the post-Napoleonic period. Human reason seemed
to have dispelled all illusions. The result was a world
crumbling to pieces. "Men doubted everything, the

young men denied everything, the poets sang of despair. The youth came from their schools with serene brows, their faces glowing with health, and blasphemy in their mouths. . . . That which was is no more; what will be is not yet. Do not seek elsewhere the cause of our malady."

Emergence of the New Social Science. The rapidly changing social structure and the ensuing climate of conflicting ideas in the nineteenth century encouraged the growth of the new social science with its will to analyze and understand. France pioneered in that respect. Tocqueville and Taine, Comte and Renan, explored the origins of contemporary society and its implications for human character and life. The great French novelists shared in this effort. No longer was the novel a mere adventure tale or a sentimental narrative; it now tried to present reality with almost scientific precision, a reality from which the author suffered and which he rejected. In subjecting contemporary society to his analysis, in unmasking the innermost and secret aspirations and motivations of its members, the artist took his revenge. In the hands of the masters of French literature the prose novel now acquired equal status with the older and more poetic forms of literature, the lyrics, the epos, and the drama.

The Revolt against Tradition. Henri Beyle (1783-1842), who wrote under the name of Stendhal, aspired to present in *Le Rouge et le Noir* (1830) "a chronicle of the nineteenth century," of the remnants of the *ancien régime,* the nobility and the priesthood, and of the ambitions animating the young generation which was inspired by the ruthless will to power of Napoleon. The novel wished to portray *la verité, l'âpre verité* (the truth, the bitter truth), and to tear away the veil of illusions. Honoré Balzac (1799-1850), less acute but more imaginative than Stendhal, created in his many novels an encyclopedia of all the characters and changes of the human life of his time. He consciously wished to write a summa of the post-Napoleonic era, as Dante had written a summa of the Middle Ages, a *Human Comedy* of a secularized society, as Dante had written the *Divine Comedy* of the age of faith. It has been rightly said of

Balzac that he discovered the importance of the private life for history. Politically he was an ultra-Royalist. He despised the new bourgeois society and saw the dissolution of all virtues and values under the influence of money and greed. He dreamed of a dictatorial and authoritarian monarchy that would combine the traditional stability of the *ancien régime* with the dynamic energy of a Napoleon. He felt that the Revolution had inaugurated an era in which mediocrity triumphed over virtue and value.

Gustave Flaubert (1821-1880), a greater artist than Stendhal or Balzac, was less concerned with political ideas, yet his hatred and contempt for the bourgeois world was even greater. He fled from society into the world of art, where he tried to conquer the banality of life by the achievement of pure form. In his hands the novel became as rigorously composed a work of art as a classical play. His unceasing efforts were directed toward finding the one exact word to reveal and expose human behavior. Flaubert in the novel and Mallarmé in poetry expressed the highest attainment of the dedication of the artist to pure art, to the cult of the word, with all its exacting discipline. In 1857 Flaubert's best known novel, *Madame Bovary,* was published. The hypocritical régime—for neither the court nor the society of the Second Empire lived according to the moral standards of Victorian England—indicted the novel for immorality. In the same year, the same fate befell the *Fleurs du Mal,* a book of poetry by Charles Baudelaire (1821-1867), who through his art and attitudes wrote one of the important chapters in the history of the modern French mind. His poems expressed the two contradictory sentiments about life revealed in much of modern French poetry, its horror and its ecstasy. The former expressed itself as *l'ennui,* the spiritual apathy, the inner chaos, which Baudelaire thought characteristic of modern man; the latter appeared as *l'ivresse,* the state of intoxication, of heightened energy, which Baudelaire sought by every possible means. With him, the boredom was naturally there; ecstasy had to be artificially produced. Both were equally remote from the normal life of the average man, "the philistine" with his middle-class mores of compromise and comfort. The bourgeois who seemed to be able to bear common life and even to enjoy it, unaware of its horrors and ecstasies, was to Baudelaire the great and despicable enemy. In his political philosophy Baudelaire was influenced by the thought of de Maistre; in his artistic attitudes he was inspired by the work of Edgar Allan Poe, whom he regarded as his master and whom he translated into French. Baudelaire did not see beauty in nature, as the eighteenth century had done, nor did he find beauty in Christianity as Chateaubriand had. To Baudelaire, human nature and nature in general seemed vitiated by sin, an abomination. Only the artistic and the artificial were worthy of praise. Baudelaire's political views, like those of Balzac, were a violent rejection of democracy. "There is nothing great among men," Baudelaire wrote in his *Intimate Journal* which he called *My Heart Laid Bare*, "except the poet, the priest, and the soldier: the man who sings, the man who blesses, and the man who sacrifices others and himself. The rest are made for the whip."

Most of modern French poetry acknowledges Baudelaire as its ancestor. Two younger poets who were only recently recognized as patron saints of modern French art, and whose brief and strange lives are still surrounded by legends, went even further than Baudelaire in their revolt against modern civilization and bourgeois society. Isadore Ducasse, who wrote under the name of Comte de Lautréamont and who died in 1870 at the age of twenty-four, left *Les Chants de Maldoror*, a novel of terror, attacking God and man alike, the hero of which represents the spirit of evil and the triumph of the unconscious. Equally violent in the glorification of the instinctive forces of man's primitive nature, but an incomparably greater poet, was Arthur Rimbaud, a decade younger than Ducasse. Rimbaud wrote some of the most famous poems in the French language before he was nineteen. Then he turned forever from literature and civilization to the restless life of an adventurer in exotic countries. After solitary years in remote Ethiopia, Rimbaud died in 1891 at the age of thirty-seven.

These poets represented the mood of a generation in revolt. One of them coined the name *poètes maudits* (cursed poets) whose guiding symbol was Lucifer, the revolting angel. They wished to master life through the magic of new and unheard of experiences communicated through a new language. They set out in a drunken boat —the title of Rimbaud's most famous poem, *Le Bateau Ivre*, which he wrote at the age of seventeen—to explore uncharted seas of human life and sensibility. Like Baudelaire, but with more brutality and vigor, Rimbaud rejected the conventional life of middle-class society. In a "season in hell" he experienced all the torments and all the ecstasies of a life "unperverted" by civilization and Christian morality and restored to the innocence of childhood or of primitive mankind. In the conception of a primitive life, in his rejection of civilization, Rimbaud resembled Rousseau. But they differed greatly: the eighteenth-century thinker dreamed of an idyllic state of nature of benign benevolence and Christian virtue; the nature which the modern poet glorified was savage and violent, anti-Christian, "beyond good and evil." Rousseau protested against the over-civilized court society of his time. Rimbaud's work and life were protests against existence itself, as Christianity and middle-class society had shaped it. He longed for a reality of life of infinitely greater intensity and in that resembled Nietzsche. "It would be difficult," writes C. A. Hackett, a contemporary literary historian, "to over-estimate the influence of Rimbaud on French literature, directly through his poetry and indirectly through the enigma and mystery of his life. He seems in the brief space of three or four years to have brilliantly used every technical device and every poetic form and to have announced most of the themes of contemporary poetry. Rimbaud's search for an inner sanction in a civilization where the traditional values are failing remains a central problem of our age."

Accent on Naturalism. The trend of the French novel in analyzing and criticizing contemporary French society was continued by Emile Zola (1840-1902). He did not follow Flaubert in that artist's dedication to art for its own sake or in his indefatigable pursuit of the perfect expression, but he shared the earlier novelist's desire to attain a scrupulously truthful portraiture of life. In his series of novels *Les Rougon Macquart*, Zola emulated Balzac in attempting to present an entire society, this time that of the Second Empire. Drawing on the methods of positivist scientific analysis introduced by Comte and Taine, Zola wrote "the natural and social history of a family," without "Victorian" inhibitions in delineating the more sordid aspects of life and society. Sharply critical of the industrial and financial capitalism which was fast encroaching upon French life, Zola did not withdraw into despairing and disdainful isolation like Flaubert, nor did he turn to the *ancien régime* as Balzac had. Zola's "naturalism" had greater social than artistic influence in France. And in his republican sympathies he could be compared to Victor Hugo, the representative of an older generation, whose survival into the times of the Third Republic carried forward some of the enthusiasms of the Napoleonic legend and 1848 into the more sober age after 1870.

Ferment in the Fine Arts. As in literature, similar trends expressed themselves in the painting of the period. Romantic poetry had found its counterpart in the art of Eugène Delacroix (1799-1863), while the sharp reaction against bourgeois society was reflected in the satirical cartoons which Honoré Daumier (1808-1879) drew for the widely read *Charivari*. Flaubert's realism may be compared to that of Gustave Courbet (1819-1877), and young Zola was united in close personal friendship with Edouard Manet (1832-1883) and Paul Cézanne (1839-1906). Their contemporary in the field of sculpture was François Auguste Rodin (1814-1917). These and other artists made Paris in the later nineteenth century a center of the arts comparable to Italy and the Netherlands in the Renaissance.

Reaction against Science and Progress. One of Zola's disciples who, however, abandoned the naturalist school to follow new paths was Joris Karl Huysmans (1848-1907). His novel *À Rebours* (1884) initiated the decadent school with its "delicious malady of the rare and the precious," a school whose most prominent English representative was Oscar Wilde. Huysmans himself traveled the road from decadence through the exploration of satanism and of occult magic in his novel *Là Bas* (1891) to the Catholic faith. He described this spiritual journey in *En Route* (1894), in which he paid homage to the beauty of the liturgic revival in the French church. The conversion of the former "naturalist" was characteristic of a growing traditionalism which became one of the main French intellectual and literary movements at the end of the nineteenth century. The optimistic faith in science and progress was no longer fashionable. On January 1, 1895, the famous *Revue des Deux Mondes* printed an article by its editor Ferdinand Brunetière (1849-1906), which proclaimed "the bankruptcy of science." Paul Bourget (1852-1935), a widely read psychological novelist, in 1889 published a novel, *Le Disciple,* which called for a return to the old faith and to the moral standards of an authoritarian society. Its hero, Robert Greslou, like Stendhal's Julien Sorel in *Le Rouge et le Noir,* or like Dostoevsky's Raskolnikov in *Crime and Punishment,* exemplified the nefarious influence of the moral "irresponsibility" prevailing in a secular society. Bourget dedicated the book to the young men of France and warned them against the dangers of materialism and dilettantism, of pure art or pure science indifferent to moral considerations. Bourget defended the bourgeoisie, the class in control, and he only regretted that it had not found the way back to monarchy and religion. On the whole, the bourgeoisie did not heed this recall to the principles of Bossuet. Its favorite author was Anatole France (1844-1924) who renewed the serene skepticism of Voltaire and the learned irony of Renan. Yet among young French intellectuals, there were a surprising number of conversions to Catholicism. Two cases which attracted special attention at the beginning of the twentieth century were those of Jacques Maritain (b. 1882), a Protestant and the grandson of Jules Favre (1809-1880) who had been one of the most ardent republican French statesmen, and that of Ernest Psichari (1883-1914), the grandson of Ernest Renan.

The Zealous Search for New Forms. The end of the nineteenth century also saw in France a great creative fermentation in all the arts. Great poets like Stéphane Mallarmé (1842-1898) and Paul Valéry (1871-1945) continued the tradition of formal perfection and poetic purity. More characteristic of this time, however, was a dissolution of classical form. Symbolism stressed the affinity of poetry and music. Through the power of symbols, poetry became a means of communication with the spiritual world behind the visible, and the poet became the interpreter of the unseen. Symbolism revived the lore of ancient creeds and myths and thus placed the experience of the poet in a timeless and legendary world. Through the complexity of forms and colors, allusions and references, the poet tried to partake of the mystery of life and of the divine. In painting and sculpture, non-objective art made its appearance. In 1911 the first exhibition of cubist painting was held in Paris. The beauty of primitive Negro art was discovered in the last years before the First World War. During the war Dadaism raised furious protestation against all aspects of "stupid" bourgeois society. After the war surrealism succeeded Dadaism in the rejection of traditional values. It was deeply influenced by the new psychology of the Viennese neurologist Sigmund Freud, whose interpretation of dreams appeared in 1900. Freud emphasized the influence of the subconscious on conscious life, the importance of early childhood with its sexuality, and the significance of the logic of the dream world. The surrealists attempted to fuse the two realities of the dream world and the actual world into some kind of absolute reality, *surrealité*, in which all the restraints and controls of reason were removed from thought and its expression in literature and art.

Thus art became the standard-bearer of permanent revolt, bent upon the destruction of all established conventions. It was, as with Rimbaud, a means of charting the unexplored continent of the subconscious mind, and its wonderland of dreams and hallucinations. According to the surrealist leader André Breton (b. 1896), literature was to be freed from its logical confines. Art was but a means to an end, and that end was a total revolution of the spirit. Surrealism aimed at the "fashioning of the collective myth" and recognized the "class war as a source of essential moral values." Though the achievements of the surrealists in the various fields of art were of minor value, surrealist theory was significant for an understanding of a period in which most French intellectuals and writers espoused extreme positions. Atheism and orthodox traditionalism, communism and fascism, found many adherents among French intellectuals and derived their inspiration from Rome and Moscow and even from Germany. After the Second World War surrealism gave way to existentialism, a movement clearly influenced by central European thinkers and poets—Hölderlin, Kierkegaard, Kafka and Heidegger—and one which reflected man's situation in an apparently hopeless and meaningless world, full of anxiety. But it would be misleading to conclude from the deep moral crisis of intellectual France that the political and social foundations of the nation were similarly shaken. Though for a long time the crisis symptoms have been grave and reforms overdue, behind the surface of ever-changing ministries and extremist trends, French society has shown a great resilience and an ability to accept common-sense solutions.

— 7 —

CONTEMPORARY FRANCE

Background of Antagonisms.   Modern France began with the French Revolution; contemporary France with the Dreyfus Affair. This affair sharply expressed all the great conflicts which had divided France since the Revolution, and it foreshadowed the critical tensions of the twentieth century. The republican régime in France seemed firmly established by the mid-eighties, but the next decade, which immediately preceded the Dreyfus Affair, was one of disturbance and agitation. There were many sources of this unrest. The working class still suffered from the defeat and suppression of the Commune. Paul Déroulède (1846-1914), whose *Chants du soldat* (1872) made him very popular, in 1882 founded the *Ligue des patriotes,* a fervently nationalistic organization which attempted to arouse the spirit of revenge against Germany. Déroulède supported General Georges Boulanger (1837-1891) as an embodiment of the spirit of revenge. Boulanger, the "man on horseback," the handsome soldier and fierce orator, won the hearts of the masses. In January 1889 he was simultaneously elected deputy in Paris and in several *départements;* everyone expected him to use his popularity for a coup d'état to overthrow the régime. But the French republicans closed ranks as they had done against MacMahon; supported by this *Union des gauches,* the government acted quickly, and Boulanger fled abroad. In the same year a magnificent world fair in Paris celebrated the Centenary of the Revolution, and on that occasion the European Social-Democratic parties formed the Second International of the working class.

Yet the newly affirmed prestige of the republican parliament suffered grievously in the Panama scandal, a financial affair which in 1892 involved many deputies. The discontent was fanned by the Rightist defamation of republican parliamentarianism as something fundamentally un-French, due to Anglo-Saxon, Protestant, or Jewish influences. The anti-Semitic agitation, begun by Edouard Drumont, who in 1886 published *La France Juive,* was supported by influential sections of the Catholic church. Some members of the Catholic hierarchy even went as far as to uphold the authenticity of the fantasies of Leo Taxil, who explained the French Revolution and every other "evil" as the work of Freemasons and Anglo-Saxons, Protestants and Jews. From there it was only a short step to the supposition of a "great Jewish plot" directed against France and her religion. Were not the Jews the people of Judas? On February 5, 1898, the official organ of the Jesuit Order in Rome maintained that the Jews should never have been granted French citizenship. "The Jews are masters of the Republic; it is not so much French as Jewish." Religious intolerance extended itself to nationalist agitation. Would not the Jewish race of traitors serve German aims and undermine the security of France?

The Dreyfus Affair.   Seen against this background of antagonisms, it becomes understandable that the question of the guilt of Captain Alfred Dreyfus shook French society to its very depths. Dreyfus, the only Jewish officer on the French general staff, was sentenced in 1894 for pro-German espionage. The French high command insisted on his guilt. For more than a decade this case split the French nation into two bitterly warring camps. The issue at stake went far beyond the fate of an individual. It engendered the most vigorous debate conducted anywhere about the nature of modern society, the claims of established authority and national interest against the rights of the individual and the objectivity of justice. Against Dreyfus were the forces of the *ancien régime*— church, army, and aristocracy—and the new nationalist emotionalism of the masses. If Dreyfus was innocent, then the French army was dishonored and stood accused of intrigues and worse. And in the tense international situation the security of France depended on the prestige of the army. Was it right to endanger it? Against this position of national interest, some intellectuals, initially fighting for objective justice and truth, succeeded in rallying the anti-clerical, anti-militarist and anti-monarchist sentiments of the French liberal tradition.

The intellectual leaders of the anti-Dreyfusards were Charles Maurras (1868-1952) and Maurice Barrès (1862-1923). They were the first to formulate clearly the principles of integral nationalism, which rejected liberal democracy, its methods of discussion, and tolerance in favor of exclusive national self-interest and speedy, decisive action. Maurras opposed the appeal to reason and universal values of the intellectuals who defended Dreyfus. He emphasized French action, *action française*. He demanded action, not deliberation, *France d'abord* (France First), not humanitarian considerations. Maurras' political goal was the restoration of the monarchy and the *ancien régime,* a situation which he desired to bring about not by parliamentary majority decisions but by the determined action of a closely knit, disciplined and well-armed vanguard, an élite which would seize leadership in a decisive moment. Like de Maistre, Maurras saw in the Roman church and in the French monarchy the bulwarks against social disorder. Church and monarchy also presented for these men an opposition to the anarchist values of the Hebrew prophets, the German Reformation, and Rousseau.

Barrès did not wish to return to the *ancien régime:* he knew that this was impossible in the age of the masses. He accepted the republic but rejected the liberal tradition and parliamentary democracy. He followed the Napoleonic tradition in seeking a personal embodiment of the true will of the people, a leader in closest touch with the life and feelings of the masses. Modern democratic nations, Barrès thought, were torn by conflicting interests and opinions and undermined by intellectualism and cosmopolitanism. The solution was to be found in a close national community of thought and feeling, which must fuse all the classes through the recognition of their common deep roots in past generations and in the ancestral soil. In his novel *Les Déracinés* (1897) Barrès castigated the uprootedness of modern intellectuals. The individual to him was merely a link in the chain of generations, inevitably determined by the blood of his forefathers.

The anti-Dreyfusards united in the *Ligue de la Patrie Française;* the Dreyfusards formed the *Ligue des Droits de l'Homme et du Citoyen.* Among the latter's leaders were Georges Clemenceau (1841-1929) and Jean Jaurès (1859-1914). Clemenceau's life was an incessant struggle for liberty and justice. He had upheld the republican tradition during the reign of Napoleon III; he had viewed the Commune with sympathy but shrank from its excesses; after 1871 he combined the radicalism of the republican Left with an unwavering French patriotism. Faithful to the liberal tradition, he saw the future of France as closely connected with Britain and the English-speaking world. Jaurès was by training a philosopher and by inclination a historian. In his doctoral dissertation, written in Latin, he dealt with the manifestations of socialism in Kant, Fichte, and Hegel, and he contrasted French distrust of the state and insistence upon individual liberty with German veneration for the state. He soon joined the French moderate socialists who were opposed to the Marxism and the intransigence of the group led by Jules Guesde (1845-1922). In 1904 Jaurès succeeded in uniting the various factions of French socialism and founded, together with Aristide Briand (1862-1932), the daily newspaper *L'Humanité*. The name he chose was characteristic of his ideas. Jaurès was a French democrat and humanitarian who abhorred violence among nations and classes and who worked throughout for unity and conciliation, in theory and in practice. He wished to make the bourgeoisie understand and accept the new rights of the proletariat—an effort in which, unfortunately, he failed—and to make the proletariat understand and accept the universal and lasting elements in the liberal tradition. In his interpretation of history Jaurès sought a synthesis of Marx's economic materialism with Michelet's moral idealism.

The Dreyfus Affair ended with the victory of the Dreyfusards. As on previous occasions, the excesses of the reactionary forces had revitalized and unified the republicans. But with victory much of the idealist fervor disappeared. The victors now used the political machine to their own advantage. They were determined to break the political power of the church. Many of the Catholic orders were disbanded. The separation of church and state was accomplished. The republican wrath turned not only against the church but also against the army high command which had largely supported the anti-Dreyfusards. The new government was staunchly republican, anti-clerical, and pacifist. Its policy of retrenchment on military expenditures and concentration on domestic issues received a rude shock in the first Morocco Crisis of 1905. Germany exploited—or so it seemed to patriotic Frenchmen—France's unpreparedness by forcing the dismissal of Théophile Delcassé (1852-1923) who as French foreign minister had forged the Anglo-French Entente Cordiale and who had helped to replace the long-standing Anglo-French rivalry with the coöperation of the two Western powers.

New Mood of Faith and Vitality: Péguy. The year 1905 marked a turning point in the mood of French youth. The change was perhaps most clearly expressed in the attitude of Charles Péguy (1873-1914). Born in Orléans, Péguy grew up in poverty. As a student he had been one of the most ardent Dreyfusards. Disappointed with the aftermath of the affair, in 1900 he founded the *Cahiers de la Quinzaine,* of which he was publisher, editor, printer, business manager, and chief contributor. In this periodical he subjected the intellectual and political trends of contemporary France to close scrutiny. A solitary man with the spirit of a moral crusader, he maintained his detachment from all the possible corruptions of society. Against Maurras but also against the politicians of the Left, he stressed the primacy of morality and disinterested truth. The *Cahiers,* produced with the same care which medieval craftsmen devoted to their work, and opposed to the commercialism and publicity of modern times, had an influence on French youth far beyond its limited circulation. Péguy had been a republican and a Socialist. He now became a Christian, reconverted to the Catholicism of his birth. But he remained a republican and a Socialist, and he was all these in a very personal, independent way. An individualist dedicated to liberty and truth, Péguy united the often conflicting French traditions of the revolutionary proletariat and the conservative peasantry in his person. He rejected the separation between the Catholic tradition of France and the spirit of 1789, between the saints of the Faith and the heroes of the Revolution. The year 1905 was a turning point for him too, as he began to stress more and more the need for patriotism. At the outbreak of the war he joined his infantry regiment and fell in the battle of the Marne. Since then he has been the greatest single influence on French youth. His life of Franciscan simplicity and poverty, his ascetic dedication to his craft and his causes, have become almost legendary.

None has invoked the idealism of the original Dreyfusards, their courage in obeying their individual consciences against the pressures of special interests, better than Péguy in his *Notre Jeunesse:* "To risk everything for Dreyfus," he wrote in his characteristic style, "all the money which one had earned so miserably, all the money of the little man, all one's time, all one's career, all one's health, body and soul, the dislocation of families, the hostility of one's relatives, the silent reprobation, the rupture of friendships of twenty years' duration. One's whole social life. The entire life of one's heart. In one word, everything. To renounce for this man peace of mind. Not only the peace of the state, of the home, of the family, but the peace of mind, the greatest good, the only good. The courage to enter for this man into the kingdom of an incurable inquietude. And of a bitterness which will never heal." That was what entering the Dreyfus controversy meant at a time when only a few intellectuals dared to raise a voice against the general trend. Looking back on the Affair, Péguy asked himself the question, whether in view of some of the consequences of the Dreyfusard victory, the struggle had been justified; whether the intellectuals, who were accused of risking the security of state and army on behalf of individual justice, had been true patriots. "A nation is something unique," he wrote, "a gigantic assemblage of the most legitimate, the most sacred rights and interests. Millions of lives depend on it in the present, the past, and the future. It is of infinite price, because it can be made and realized only once. The first duty of so unique an achievement is not to let itself be jeopardized for one man, whoever he may be, however legitimate his interest. Dreyfus had to be sacrificed if need be for the repose and safety of France. So some said. But we answered that a single injustice, a single illegality, especially if it be officially confirmed, a single insult offered to justice and to right, especially if it be generally, nationally, conveniently accepted, is enough to dishonor and disgrace an entire nation. It is a gangrenous spot which soon spreads over the whole body." The France for which Péguy stood insisted on the personal responsibility and the importance of the individual and on the objective pursuit of truth.

There was an element of the heroic in Péguy's life and thought which was characteristic of a new mood in France, an attitude in which the former prevailing skepticism, positivism, and defeatism gave way to faith, vitality, and a new seriousness. Péguy revered the French philosopher Henri Bergson (1859-1941) and his struggle against the ossification of life, his appeal to spiritual greatness. To the theories of mechanical evolution widely accepted in the second half of the nineteenth century, Bergson opposed his concept of creative evolution and of intuitive understanding. Instead of seeking the origins of life in the mechanical and inorganic, he defined the mechanical as the product of the decay and failure of life, whose essence he believed to be spontaneous creativeness. Bergson's *élan vital* came as an inspiration to an enervated generation. In 1903 Romain Rolland (1866-1945) published in Péguy's *Cahiers de la Quinzaine* a "heroic biography" of Beethoven. Like Péguy and Bergson, Romain Rolland suffered under the then-prevailing gloom and indifference. "The air around us is heavy," he wrote in the book's introduction; "the old Europe is benumbed in a sluggish and vicious atmosphere. A materialism without grandeur oppresses thought and fetters the action of government and individuals. The world dies of suffocation in its prudent and vile egoism; the world is stifling. Let us open the windows. Let free air enter. Let us partake of the breath of heroes."

New Ethics of Violence: Sorel. The feeling of a crisis in morality and society led some French thinkers to extremist positions. The nationalist conception of Barrès was paralleled by the revolutionary mythology of Georges Sorel (1847-1922) whose *Reflections on Violence* appeared in 1906. Sorel rejected the "illusion" of an inevitable progress. Like Nietzsche, he diagnosed the malady of his time as a moral crisis due to the decadence of the democratic élite, a decadence inherent, according to Sorel, in the nature of parliamentary democracy itself. A new order had to be imposed by the heroic action of a conspiratorial élite, a group bound together in fervent solidarity against the rest of society and passionately confident of its ultimate triumph. Like Maurras or Lenin, Sorel repudiated the democratic process of negotiation and compromise and the integration of all classes and interests, in spite of their differences, into one greater whole. Democracy, which tends to reduce differences and to lessen antagonisms, he believed to be a weakener of the moral fibre of society, and he insisted that only relentless conflict could bring forth those virtues without which no regeneration was possible.

Like Robespierre, Sorel was a puritan who believed that extreme means must be utilized to make men virtuous. Like Michelet, he regarded military heroism and sublime group patriotism as supreme virtues. The bourgeois world seemed to him to perish in fear and cowardice in the pursuit of petty goals of self-gratification. Like the French traditionalists, Sorel was repelled by the vulgarity and sentimentality of the democratic age and magnified the strength of the élites of the *ancien régime*. He was a revolutionary and an authoritarian. At a time when many believed in the continuing spread of Western ways of liberal democracy and social reform all over the earth, Sorel called for a total transformation of society by the ruthless seizure of power by a group inspired, as Sorel said, by a "myth." In his definition, such a myth was to give an aspect of complete reality to the hopes aroused by immediate action. The myth need bear no relation to factual truth; it must express the deep but inarticulate desire of the masses, arouse memories of past conflicts, and encourage unyielding loyalty. It must be simple, it must focus on the immediate need of destroying the existing social order, and it must provide the incentive to heroic deeds. The test of a myth was to be found in its power to influence action. "To discuss how far it can be taken literally as future history is devoid of sense." For, said Sorel, myths are "not descriptions of things but expressions of a determination to act." Thus they can neither be proven nor refuted.

Sorel looked to the proletariat as the agents of salvation and to the general strike as the new myth. Proletarian violence inspired by this myth, he hoped, would redeem the world from bourgeois decadence and might even succeed in restoring to the middle class some of its former energies. To that end, an élite composed of the most audacious vanguard of the proletariat, conscious of its superior merit, but in accord with the innermost instincts of the masses, should impose itself upon the entire working class. Thus proletarian violence would be at the service of civilization itself. "Perhaps it is not the most appropriate manner of obtaining immediate material advantages, but it may save the world from barbarism." (*See Reading No. 21.*)

In his last years, Sorel witnessed Lenin and Mussolini make use of myths in their successful coups which, on the whole, followed his direction for the leadership of violent élites. In 1919, in the appendix to a new edition of *Reflections on Violence,* Sorel hailed Lenin for replacing the impotent commercial civilization of the bourgeois democracies by the heroic civilization of the Russian proletariat. "New Carthages must not triumph over what is now the Rome of the proletariat." Two years later Sorel added, to his admiration of this "Third Rome" in Moscow, an enthusiasm for the "Third Rome" on the banks of the Tiber. Fascists and Communists alike seemed to him to represent the aggressive élite from whom he expected the regeneration of civilization. In his life and thought Sorel expressed the alienation of many French intellectuals from modern society and their faith in the magic efficacy of revolution.

The Cry for Peace: Jaurès. Against this summons to violence, Jaurès maintained the French *sens de mesure.* After 1905 when the atmosphere in Europe grew continually heavier, he turned more and more to the problems of international relations and the preservation of peace. (*See Reading No. 22.*) His pacifism did not lead him to the espousal of complete disarmament. "A nation which could not count, in days of crisis or when its life is in danger, upon the national devotion of its working class, would be a wretched thing indeed." Like William James, Jaurès was convinced of the need for a "moral equivalent to war." Jaurès warned that love of peace does not demand less courage than the pursuit of war. "Courage means," he told the French youth in 1903, "to seek and speak the truth, not to succumb to the passing triumph of untruths and not to echo the cheers of foolish crowds and the jeers of the fanatics." As a democrat and as a patriot Jaurès did everything in his power to avert the threatening danger of war. When his impassioned efforts failed, he would undoubtedly have rallied to the military defense of France, *dont le fier génie est ce qu'il y a de meilleur en nous* ("whose proud genius is the best part of ourselves"), but on the

very eve of mobilization, July 31, 1914, Jaurès was
assassinated by a nationalist fanatic. His death was a loss
to the cause of peace and democracy. Had he lived, he
would have kept the French workers in the Western fold;
but with Jaurès gone, the majority of the French Socialist
Party in 1921 decided to join the Communist International directed from Moscow. Working-class unity and
national unity were thus dealt a heavy blow in a critical
hour.

The Impact of World War I.   The First World War
undermined the moral texture of Europe. One of the nations most deeply hurt was France. The flower of her
younger generation was killed, and the effort of a four
years' defense against Germany proved too great a strain
for her. She was saved from defeat only by the coöperation of Britain and the United States. The unity of the
three democracies won the war: it could have preserved
the peace. The Western world, strongly unified and
secure in its position, could have integrated Germany
into the Western community and thereby halted the
inroads of those anti-Western movements, Communism
and Fascism, which felt that the twentieth century belonged to them and that the West was in an inevitable
decline. Unfortunately, Clemenceau alone among the
peacemakers understood the need for close coöperation
between France and her Western allies in order to
guarantee the security and stability of the ever-threatened
cornerstone of democracy on the European continent.
The United States and Britain refused her coöperation.
France was left to herself with her energies sapped and
with a growing feeling of insecurity. Far from being
integrated into the Western community, Germany was
left to follow her deeply seated anti-Western traditions
to their logical conclusion in the Second World War. In
France the urgent social task of full integration into
national society of the new social strata created by the
industrial revolution was not accomplished. The decline
of France, however, was less apparent in the years after
the First World War because France was living through
one of her most fertile and exciting cultural periods.
Paris again became the place of pilgrimage for eager
students of literature and the arts. An unprecedented

mastery of the realistic novel and a simultaneous dissolution of its form was revealed in the work of Marcel Proust (1871-1922). The Catholic dogma was magnificently brought to poetic life by Paul Claudel (b. 1868). The individual Protestant conscience with its doubts and torments was vividly and sincerely presented by André Gide (1869-1951). But in the midst of this splendid intellectual and cultural effervescence, one of the great masters of France, Paul Valéry, in an address delivered shortly after the end of the war, warned:

"The storm has died away, and still we are restless, uneasy, as if the storm were about to break. Almost all the affairs of men remain in a terrible uncertainty. We think of what has disappeared, we are almost destroyed by what has been destroyed; we do not know what will be born, and we fear the future, not without reason. We hope vaguely, we dread precisely; our fears are infinitely more precise than our hopes; we confess that the charm of life is behind us, abundance is behind us, but doubt and disorder are in us and with us. There is no thinking man, however shrewd or learned he may be, who can hope to dominate this anxiety, to escape from this impression of darkness, to measure the probable duration of this period when the vital relations of humanity are disturbed profoundly.

"One can say that all the fundamentals of our world have been affected by the war, or more exactly, by the circumstances of the war; something deeper has been worn away than the renewable parts of the machine. You know how greatly the general economic situation has been disturbed, and the polity of states, and the very life of the individual; you are familiar with the universal discomfort, hesitation, apprehension. But among all these injured things is the Mind. The Mind has indeed been cruelly wounded; its complaint is heard in the hearts of intellectual man; it passes a mournful judgment on itself. It doubts itself profoundly."

Military and Moral Collapse: World War II. The years preceding the Second World War revealed how deeply the French mind doubted itself. Fascism and Communism sapped its strength. Faced in 1939 with German aggression, France was neither united nor strong enough to resist effectively. The British and American help, which Clemenceau had rightly believed indispensable, came too late. France collapsed militarily and morally. Paris, which had resisted the German armies for four months in 1870 and borne all the privations of a long siege, surrendered to the enemy without a shot. The heroic stories of Madrid, London, or Leningrad found no counterpart in France. In the general pusillanimity, the French government in 1940 lacked the courage and foresight to accept the offer of the British government under Winston Churchill that a Franco-British union be created for the continuation of the war. The French government surrendered. The majority of the French nation turned trustfully to the aged Marshal Henri Pétain (1856-1952). Pétain and his followers were inspired by the ideas of Charles Maurras: they glorified the "virtues" of the *ancien régime* and despised parliamentary democracy and the liberal tradition. They hated England and had no doubt that she was doomed and that the "wave of the future" coming from the East would engulf the whole of Europe.

British resistance decided otherwise. The armies of the Western democracies liberated France. They were supported by growing numbers of Frenchmen who, abroad and at home, shook off the torpor which had numbed the nation. Under their leadership the Fourth Republic emerged in 1944. At the beginning, its character was undefined. The legend of the *ancien régime* which Pétain had tried to revive seemed finally discredited. But the vicissitudes of the war brought other trends into the spotlight. General Charles de Gaulle appealed to the heroic virtues and the military spirit of the French tradition, to Joan of Arc and Napoleon. Many members of the Resistance were inspired by the revolutionary tradition of Babeuf and of the Commune. Their eyes were directed toward Moscow. Yet very soon, the Fourth Republic came most closely to resemble the Third Republic. Since 1879 the liberal tradition and the republican régime have shown more coherence than is generally assumed, and this is equally true of France since 1945. Ever endangered by the absolutism of the *ancien régime* and by the impatient fervor of social utopias and collective glory, France has remained faithful to the critical individualism and the humane tolerance of modern Western civilization.

The Second World War left France far more exhausted than the First World War. It would be wrong and dangerous, however, to overestimate her weakness—too much of the future of freedom on the continent depends on France. Many of her intellectuals are painfully disoriented. But their predicament is neither new nor unique. Many observers have compared the present time to that of the decadence of the ancient Graeco-Roman civilization; many again believe that the new scientific discoveries threaten man. But more than a century ago we find the bishop in Stendhal's *Le Rouge et le Noir* saying, "The end of pagan antiquity was accompanied by a state of mind of restlessness and doubt, the same which now in the nineteenth century desolates our sad and bored minds." The philosophical poet of Stendhal's generation, Alfred de Vigny (1797-1863) in his *Daphné,* compared the decomposition of the ancient world with the anarchy of values in his society. Vigny's Libanius sees the remedy in an appeal to the barbarians who have something more precious than all the scholarship of the ages, which they will bring to the disintegrating world: simplicity and strength of faith, the certainty of something miraculous, a morality not sapped by doubts and sophistry. And Vigny expressed too, as early as 1842, the feeling of man's helplessness before the machines which he has created—a feeling so predominant in the middle of the twentieth century—on the occasion of a railroad accident at Versailles:

> *Tous se sont dit: Allons! Mais aucun n'est le maître*
> *Du dragon mugissant qu'un savant a fait naître.*
> *Nous nous sommes joué à plus fort que nous tous.*

(We told ourselves, let's go ahead. But none can master the roaring dragon which a scientist created. We have meddled with something that is much stronger than we all are.)

But Vigny was not frightened. He saw the dangers, but he also saw the great potentialities of the new inventions.

Beni soit le commerce au hardi caducée,
Si l'amour que tourmente une sombre pensée
Peut franchir en un jour deux grandes nations.

(Blessed be the commerce of hardy Mercury's wand,
when love which is tormented by a somber thought,
can in one day cross the frontiers of two great
nations.)

The monstrous new machines threaten man, but they
challenge and promise, too. Vigny foresaw one of their
beneficial results in 1842: that the days of the self-
sufficient nation-state are gone. France herself, through
the absolute monarchy and in the centralized state born
with the Revolution, presented the classical model of
such a nation-state. Yet in her best moments, in the
universalist and humanist character of her eighteenth-
century philosophy, France has surpassed the limitations
of the nation-state. Heir to this liberal tradition, Renan,
in an address at Oxford in 1880, emphasized that "our
nation is not everything. We are men and children of
God before being French or German. The kingdom of
God, that eternal dream which cannot be uprooted from
the heart of man, is a perpetual protest against what is
too exclusive in patriotism. The nation-state does and
can do only one thing, organize the collective selfishness.
This is not unimportant, but it is not enough."

The Burning Task of Readjustment.   France, weakened by two wars, surrounded by nations much stronger
in industrial equipment, efficiency, and man power, faces
the difficult task of readjustment to the new situation.
She must discard, in international politics and domestic
economy, cherished but outworn attitudes of the past.
Victory in the Second World War created the opportunity of bringing France and Germany closer than they
had been for the last 150 years. During that period
cultural ties existed; Michelet and Renan owed much to
Germany; Goethe, Heine, and Nietzsche acknowledged
their deep indebtedness to France. But Germany's anti-
Western attitudes turned her against her western neigh-
bor, and the memories of four German invasions in
modern times have kept fear alive in many French hearts.
In view of this past, a real rapprochement of the two

great continental nations is only possible after the forging
of those close ties between France and the English-
speaking nations, envisaged by Clemenceau after the
First World War and brought closer to realization by the
experience of the Second World War. Only if confronted
by the closest union of France with Britain and the
United States will Germany abandon her own anti-
Western traditions and sincerely desire integration into
the West. Only if fully assured of her unity with Britain
and the United States will France feel confident enough
to enter a close association with Germany. For contemporary France, the German and the Atlantic problem,
external security and internal democracy, are interde-
pendent. Close coöperation with the West, as well as
making France secure, will preserve her passion for
individual liberty. Thanks to this passion, the republic
seems secure in France today, whatever the momentary
threats of Communism or exclusive nationalism may be.
In the last lines of *Notre Jeunesse,* Péguy answered the
many doubts about the vitality of French democracy
expressed in the beginning of the twentieth century. His
answer is as valid now. In these lines, Péguy recalled the
words of a friend who, in concluding a long discussion
about the various factions menacing the existence of the
democratic republic, said: "All this is very well because
these threats are only theoretical and lack precision.
But on the day on which they will become a real
menace, they will realize what we are still capable of in
the defense of the republic."

Part II

READINGS

— Reading No. 1 —

VOLTAIRE: *THE BEGINNINGS OF THE ENLIGHTENMENT*[1]

Voltaire's experiences in England strengthened his determination to fight for political and intellectual liberty in France. In 1734 he published his *Lettres Philosophiques sur les Anglais,* which had already appeared in an English translation. The *Lettres* gave the French their first detailed knowledge of conditions across the Channel.

If one religion only were allowed in England, the government would very possibly become arbitrary; if there were but two, the people would cut one another's throats; but as there are such a multitude, they all live happy, and in peace. . . .

The members of the English Parliament are fond of comparing themselves to the old Romans.

Not long since, Mr. Shippen opened a speech in the House of Commons with these words, "the Majesty of the people of England would be wounded." The singularity of the expression occasioned a loud laugh; but this Gentleman, so far from being disconcerted, repeated the same words with a resolute tone of voice, and the laugh ceased. In my opinion, the Majesty of the people of England has nothing in common with that of the people of Rome; much less is there any affinity between their governments. There is in London a Senate, some of the members whereof are accused (doubtless very unjustly)

[1] Mr. de Voltaire, *Letters Concerning the English Nation,* New edition, London: L. Davis and C. Reymers, 1760, pp. 37, 42-46, 56-59, 177-79 (letters VI, VIII, X, XXIII).

of selling their voices on certain occasions, as was done
in Rome; this is the only resemblance. Besides, the two
nations appear to me quite opposite in character, with
regard both to good and evil. The Romans never knew
the dreadful folly of religious wars, an abomination reserved for devout preachers of patience and humility.
Marius and Sulla, Caesar and Pompey, Anthony and
Augustus, did not draw their swords and set the world
in a blaze merely to determine whether the Flamen
should wear his shirt over his robe, or his robe over
his shirt; or whether the sacred chickens should eat and
drink, or eat only, in order to take the augury. The
English have hanged one another by law, and cut one
another to pieces in pitched battles, for quarrels of as
trifling a nature. The sects of the Episcopalians and
Presbyterians quite distracted these very serious heads for
a time. But I fancy they'll hardly ever be so silly again,
they seeming to be grown wiser at their own expense; and
I don't perceive the least inclination in them to murder
one another merely about syllogisms, as some zealots
among them once did.

But here follows a more essential difference between
Rome and England, which gives the advantage entirely
to the latter, viz., that the civil wars of Rome ended in
slavery, and those of the English in liberty. The English
are the only people upon earth who have been able to
prescribe limits to the power of Kings by resisting them;
and who, by a series of struggles, have at last established
that wise government, where the prince is all-powerful
to do good, and at the same time is restrained from
committing evil; where the nobles are great without
intolerance, tho' there are no vassals; and where the
people share in the government without confusion. . . .

That which rises to a revolution in England is no
more than a sedition in other countries. A city in Spain,
in Barbary, or in Turkey, takes up arms in defence of its
privileges, when immediately it is stormed by mercenary
troops, it is punished by executioners, and the rest of
the nation kiss the chains they are loaded with. The
French are of opinion that the government of this
island is more tempestuous than the sea which surrounds
it; which indeed is true; but then it is never so but when

the King raises the storm; when he attempts to seize the ship of which he is only the chief pilot. The civil wars of France lasted longer; were more cruel, and productive of greater evils than those of England: and none of these civil wars had a wise and prudent liberty for their object. . . .

As trade enriched the citizens in England, so it contributed to their freedom, and this freedom on the other side extended their commerce, whence arose the grandeur of the state. Trade raised by insensible degrees the naval power which gives the English a superiority over the seas, and they now are masters of very near two hundred ships of war. Posterity will very possibly be surprised to hear that an island, whose only produce is a little lead, tin, fuller's earth, and coarse wool, should become so powerful by its commerce, as to be able to send, in 1723, three fleets at the same time to three different and far distanced parts of the globe. One before Gibraltar, conquered and still possessed by the English; a second to Porto Bello, to dispossess the King of Spain of the treasures of the West Indies; and a third into the Baltic, to prevent the northern powers from coming to an engagement.

At the time when Louis XIV made all Italy tremble, and his armies, which had already possessed themselves of Savoy and Piedmont, were upon the point of taking Turin, Prince Eugene was obliged to march from the middle of Germany in order to succour Savoy. Having no money, without which cities cannot be either taken or defended, he addressed himself to some English merchants. These, at an hour and a half's warning, lent him five millions, whereby he was enabled to deliver Turin, and to beat the French; after which he wrote the following short letter to the persons who had disbursed him the above-mentioned sums: "Gentlemen, I have received your money, and flatter myself that I have laid it out to your satisfaction." Such a circumstance as this raises a just pride in an English merchant and makes him presume (not without some reason) to compare himself to a Roman citizen; and indeed a peer's brother does not think traffic beneath him. When the Lord Townshend was minister of state, a brother of his was content to be a city merchant; and at the time that the Earl of Oxford governed Great Britain, his younger brother was no more than a factor in Aleppo, where he chose to live, and where he died. This custom, which begins however to be laid aside, appears monstrous to Germans, vainly puffed up with their extraction. These think it morally impossible that the son of an English peer should be no more than a rich and powerful citizen, for all are princes in Germany. There have been thirty highnesses of the same name, all whose patrimony consisted only in their escutcheons and their pride.

In France the title of marquis is given gratis to anyone who will accept it; and whosoever arrives at Paris from the midst of the most remote provinces with money in his purse, and a name terminating in *ac* or *ille,* may strut about and cry, "Such a man as I! A man of my rank and figure!" And may look down upon a trader with sovereign contempt; whilst the trader on the other side, by thus often hearing his profession treated so disdainfully, is food enough to blush at it. However, I cannot say which is most useful to a nation, a lord, powdered in the tip of the mode, who knows exactly at what a clock the king rises and goes to bed; and who gives himself airs of grandeur and state, at the same time that he is acting the slave in the anti-chamber of a prime minister; or a merchant, who enriches his country, dispatches orders from his compting-house to Surat and Grand Cairo, and contributes to the felicity of the World. . . .

Merit indeed meets in England with rewards of another kind, which redound more to the honour of the nation. The English have so great a veneration for exalted talents that a man of merit in their country is always sure of making his fortune. Mr. Addison in France would have been elected a member of one of the academies, and, by the credit of some women, might have obtained a yearly pension of twelve hundred livres; or else might have been imprisoned in the Bastille, upon pretense that certain strokes in his *Tragedy of Cato* had been discovered which glanced at the porter of some man in power. Mr. Addison was raised to the post of secretary of state in England. Sir Isaac Newton was made warden of the royal mint. Mr. Congreve had a considerable employment. Mr. Prior was plenipotentiary. Dr. Swift is Dean of St. Patrick in Dublin and is more revered in Ireland than the primate himself. The religion, which Mr. Pope professes, excludes him indeed from preferments of every kind, but then it did not prevent his gaining two hundred thousand livres by his excellent translation of Homer. I myself saw a long time in France the author of Rhadamistus ready to perish for hunger: And the son of one of the greatest men our country ever gave birth to, and who was beginning to run the noble career which his father had set him, would have been reduced to the extremes of misery, had he not been patronized by Mr. Fagon.

But the circumstance which mostly encourages the arts in England is the great veneration which is paid them. The picture of the prime minister hangs over the chimney of his own closet, but I have seen that of Mr. Pope in twenty noblemen's houses. Sir Isaac Newton was revered in his life-time and had a due respect paid to him after his death; the greatest men in the nation disputing who should have the honour of holding up his pall. Go into Westminster Abbey, and you'll find, that what raises the admiration of the spectator is not the mausoleums of the English kings, but the monuments, which the gratitude of the nation has erected to perpetuate the memory of those illustrious men who contributed to its glory. We view their statues in that abbey in the same manner as those of Sophocles, Plato, and other immortal personages were viewed in Athens; and I am persuaded that the bare sight of those glorious monuments has fired more than one breast, and been the occasion of their becoming great men.

The English have even been reproached with paying too extravagant honours to mere merit, and censured for interring the celebrated actress Mrs. Oldfield in Westminster Abbey, with almost the same pomp as Sir Isaac Newton. Some pretend that the English had paid her these great funeral honours, purposely to make us more strongly sensible of the barbarity and injustice which they object to us, for having buried Mademoiselle Le Couvreur ignominiously in the fields.

But be assured from me, that the English were prompted by no other principle, in burying Mrs. Oldfield in Westminster Abbey, than their good sense. They are far from being so ridiculous as to brand with infamy an art which has immortalized an Euripides and a Sophocles; or to exclude from the body of their citizens a set of people whose business is to set off, with the utmost grace of speech and action, those pieces which the nation is proud of.

— Reading No. 2 —

CONDORCET: *PROGRESS AND REASON* [2]

The faith of the Enlightenment found its most sublime expression in the *Esquisse d'un Tableau Historique des Progrès de l'Esprit Humain* by the Marquis de Condorcet. A scion of the ancient French nobility and a mathematician of renown, Condorcet wrote this book when he was forced to go into hiding because he opposed the Terror. The work was published after his death in 1794 and immediately translated into English.

✓   ✓   ✓

If man can predict, almost with certainty, those appearances of which he understands the laws; if, even when the laws are unknown to him, experience or the past enables him to foresee, with considerable probability, future appearances; why should we suppose it a

[2] De Condorcet, *Outlines of an Historical View of the Progress of the Human Mind,* translated from the French, Baltimore: A. Fryer, 1802, pp. 209-44.

chimerical undertaking to delineate, with some degree of truth, the picture of the future destiny of mankind from the results of its history? The only foundation of faith in the natural sciences is the principle, that the general laws, known or unknown, which regulate the phenomena of the universe, are regular and constant; and why should this principle, applicable to the other operations of nature, be less true when applied to the development of the intellectual and moral faculties of man? . . .

Our hopes, as to the future condition of the human species, may be reduced to three points: the destruction of inequality between different nations, the progress of equality in one and the same nation, and, lastly, the real improvement of man.

Will not every nation one day arrive at the state of civilization attained by those people who are most enlightened, most free, most exempt from prejudices, as the French, for instance, and the Anglo-Americans? Will not the slavery of countries subjected to kings, the barbarity of African tribes, and the ignorance of savages gradually vanish? Is there upon the face of the globe a single spot whose inhabitants are condemned by nature never to enjoy liberty, never to exercise their reason?

Does the difference of knowledge, of means, and of wealth, observable hitherto in all civilized nations, belong to civilization itself, or to the imperfections of the social order? Must not that inequality continually diminish, in order to give place to that actual equality, the chief end of the social art, which, diminishing even the effect of the natural difference of the faculties, leaves no other inequality subsisting but what is useful to the interest of all, because it will favor civilization, instruction, and industry, without drawing after it either dependence, humiliation or poverty? In a word, will not men be continually verging towards that state, in which all will possess the requisite knowledge for conducting themselves in the common affairs of life by their own reason, and of maintaining that reason uncontaminated by prejudices; in which they will understand their rights, and exercise them according to their opinion and their conscience; in which all will be able, by the development of their faculties, to procure the certain means of providing for their wants; lastly, in which folly and wretchedness will be accidents, happening only now and then, and not the habitual lot of a considerable portion of society?

Finally may it not be expected that the human race will be meliorated by new discoveries in the sciences and the arts, and, as an unavoidable consequence, in the means of individual and general prosperity; by further progress in the principles of conduct, and in moral practice; and lastly, by the real improvement of our faculties, moral, intellectual and physical, which may be the result either of the improvement of the instruments which increase the power and direct the exercise of those faculties, or of the improvement of our natural organization itself?

In examining the three questions we have enumerated, we shall find the strongest reasons to believe, from past experience, from observation of the progress which the sciences and civilization have hitherto made, and from the analysis of the march of the human understanding, and the development of its faculties, that nature has fixed no limits to our hopes. . . .

Run through the history of our projects and establishments in Africa or in Asia, and you will see our monopolies, our treachery, or sanguinary contempt for men of a different complexion or different creed, and the proselytizing fury or the intrigues of our priests, destroying that sentiment of respect and benevolence which the superiority of our information and the advantages of our commerce had at first obtained. But the period is doubtless approaching, when, no longer exhibiting to the view of these people only corrupters or tyrants, we shall become instruments of benefit to them, and the generous champions of their redemption from bondage. . . .

The march of these people will be less slow and more sure than ours has been, because they will derive from us that light which we have been obliged to discover, and because for them to acquire the simple truths and infallible methods which we have obtained after long wandering in the mazes of error, it will be sufficient to seize upon their development and proofs in our discourses and publications. When mutual wants shall have drawn

closer the ties of all mankind, and when the most powerful nations shall have established in political principles
equality between societies as well as between individuals,
and respect for the independence of feeble states, as well
as compassion for ignorance and wretchedness, will there
still be reason to fear that the globe will contain spaces
inaccessible to knowledge, or that the pride of despotism
will be able to oppose barriers to truth that will long
be insurmountable? . . .

In tracing the history of societies we have had occasion
to remark, that there frequently exist considerable distinctions between the rights which the law acknowledges
to the citizens of a state, and those which they really
enjoy. Three principal causes may be assigned for these
distinctions: inequality of wealth, inequality of condition
between him whose resources of subsistence are secured
to himself and descendable to his family, and him whose
resources are annihilated with the termination of his life,
or rather of that part of his life in which he is capable of
labor; and lastly, inequality of instruction.

It will therefore behoove us to show that these three
kinds of real inequality must continually diminish; but
without becoming absolutely extinct, since they have
natural and necessary causes, which it would be absurd
as well as dangerous to think of destroying; nor can we
attempt even to destroy entirely their effects, without
opening at the same time more fruitful sources of inequality and giving to the rights of man a more direct
and fatal blow. . . .

This inequality, however, may in great measure be
destroyed by setting chance against chance in securing to
him who attains old age a support, arising from his
savings, but augmented by those of other persons who,
making a similar addition to a common stock, may happen to die before they shall have occasion to recur to it;
in procuring, by a like regulation, an equal resource for
women who may lose their husbands, or children who
may lose their father; lastly, in preparing for those
youths who arrive at an age of work capability and of
giving birth to a new family, the benefit of a capital
sufficient to employ their industry, and increased at the
expense of those whom premature death may cut off

before they arrive at that period. To the application of mathematics to the probabilities of life and the interest of money, we are indebted for the hint of these means, already employed with some degree of success, though they have not been carried to such an extent or employed in such a variety of forms as to render them truly beneficial, not merely to a few families but to the whole mass of society which would thereby be relieved from that periodical ruin observable in a number of families, the overflowing source of corruption and depravity. . . .

We may enumerate other means of securing the equality in question, either by preventing credit from continuing to be a privilege exclusively attached to large fortunes, without at the same time placing it upon a less solid foundation; or by rendering the progress of industry and the activity of commerce more independent of the existence of great capitalists: and for these resources also we shall be indebted to the science of calculation. . . .

We might show that by a happy choice of the subjects to be taught and the mode of inculcating them, the entire mass of a people may be instructed in everything necessary for domestic economy, for the transaction of their affairs, for the free development of their industry and their faculties, for the knowledge, exercise and protection of their rights, for a sense of their duties and the power of discharging them, for the capacity of judging both their own actions and the actions of others by their own understanding, and for the acquisition of all the delicate or dignified sentiments that are an honor to humanity. . . .

The advantages that must result from the state of improvement, of which I have proved we may almost certainly entertain the hope, can have no limit but the absolute perfection of the human species; since in proportion as different kinds of equality are established to provide for our wants concerning a more universal instruction and a greater liberty, the realer will be this equality, and the closer it will approach to the fulfillment of everything important to the happiness of mankind. . . .

It will be impossible for men to become enlightened

upon the principles of morality, upon the motives for conformation to these principles, and upon their interests, whether relative to their individual or social capacity; without making at the same time an advancement in moral practice no less real than the advancement of science itself. Is not mistaken interest the most frequent cause of actions contrary to the general welfare? Is not the impetuosity of our passions the continual result either of habits to which we addict ourselves from a false calculation, or of ignorance of the means by which to resist their first impulse—to divert, govern, and direct their action? . . .

Among these causes of human improvement most important to the general welfare must be included the total annihilation of the prejudices which have established between the sexes an inequality of rights, fatal even to the sex which it favors. In vain do we search for motives to justify this principle, in differences of physical organization, of intellect or of moral sensibility. It had at first no other origin but abuse of strength, and all the attempts which have since been made to support it are idle sophisms.

And here we may observe how greatly the abolition of the usages authorized by this prejudice and of the laws which it has dictated, would tend to augment the happiness of families. It would render common the virtues of domestic life, that fountainhead of all the others; it would favor instruction and would make it truly general, either because it would be extended to both sexes with greater equality or because it could not become general even to men, without the concurrence of the mothers of families. Would it not produce what has hitherto been a mere chimera: national manners of a mild and pure nature, formed not by imperious privations, by hypocritical appearances, by reserves imposed by the fear of shame or religious terrors, but by habits freely contracted, inspired by nature and avowed by reason?

The people, being more enlightened and having resumed the right of disposing for themselves of their blood and their treasure, will learn by degrees to regard war as the most dreadful of all calamities, the most terrible of all crimes. The first wars that will be superseded will be those into which the usurpers of sovereignty have hitherto drawn their subjects for the maintenance of pretended hereditary rights.

Nations will know that they cannot become conquerors without losing their freedom; that perpetual confederations are the only means of maintaining their independence, that their object should be security and not power. By degrees commercial prejudices will die away; a false mercantile interest will lose the terrible power of soaking the earth in blood and of ruining nations under the idea of enriching them. As the people of different countries at last are drawn into closer intimacy by the principles of politics and morality; as each, for its own advantage, invites foreigners to an equal participation in the benefits which it may have derived either from nature or from its own industry; all the causes which produce, envenom, and perpetuate national animosities, will one by one disappear and will no longer furnish either fuel or pretext for warlike insanity. . . .

— Reading No. 3 —

ROBESPIERRE: *TERROR AND POLITICAL MORALITY* [3]

On February 15, 1794, Robespierre addressed the Convention on the principles of political ethics which should guide the body in governing the Republic.

ʔ　　　ʔ　　　ʔ

In our country we want morality in the place of egotism, integrity in place of honor, principles in place of habits, the rule of reason in place of the tyranny of fashion, contempt for vice in the place of contempt for misfortune, the love of glory in place of avarice. We want good men instead of "good company," merit instead of intrigue, genius instead of wit, truth instead of empty show, the charm of happiness instead of the troubles of sensual pleasures, the greatness of man instead of the meanness of the great, a magnanimous, powerful and happy people instead of an unfriendly, frivolous and unhappy one. That is to say, all the virtues and wonders of a republic in place of all the vices and the foolishness of a monarchy.

In one word, we want to fulfill nature's wishes, carry out the destiny of humanity, keep the promises of philosophy, absolve Providence from its long reign of crime and tyranny. We hope that France, which used to shine among the enslaved countries, will eclipse the glory of all the free peoples that ever lived and will become a model nation, the terror of the oppressors, the consoler of the oppressed, the ornament of the universe, and that by sealing our work with our blood we will be able to see

[3] *Discours et Rapports de Robespierre, avec une introduction et des notes par Charles Vellay,* Paris: Eugène Fasquelle, editeur, 1908. "Rapport sur les principes de morale politique qui doivent guider la Convention" (15 Fevrier, 1794), pp. 325-27, 327-28, 330-31, 332-34, 335, 345-46.

at least the dawn of universal happiness! . . . That is our ambition, and that is our goal.

What is the fundamental principle of a democratic government, the basis of its support and the mainspring of its action? It is virtue: I speak of public virtue which worked so many wonders in Greece and Rome and which will work even greater ones in republican France: I speak of that virtue which is nothing else but the love of one's country and its laws!

Since equality is the essence of a republic or a democracy, it follows that the love for country necessarily includes the love of equality.

It is also true that this sublime sentiment presupposes a preference for the public interest over all private interests; here we see again that the love for country presupposes or produces all virtues; don't virtues give strength to the soul and enable it to render these sacrifices? How, for example, could the slave of avarice or of ambition offer his idol to his country?

Virtue is not only the soul of a democracy, it could not even exist outside of such a government. Only one individual in a monarchy can love his country, and with him it need not be a virtue; that is the monarch. This is so because of all the inhabitants of the State, the monarch is the only one who has a *patrie*. Isn't he in fact the sovereign? Consequently, in aristocratic states, the word *patrie* means something only to a few patrician families who partake of its sovereignty.

Only in a democracy can all the individuals who make up the state call it their *patrie;* thus only a democracy can count on as many interested defenders of its cause as it has citizens. That is why a free people is superior to all other people. That is the reason why Athens and Sparta triumphed over the Asian tyrants, and the Swiss were victorious over the Spanish and Austrian tyrants.

However, the French are the first people in the world to have established a true democracy, since they have proclaimed the equality of man and have given the citizen his full rights; therefore, in my opinion, all the tyrants who have allied themselves against the republic will be defeated. . . .

Luckily, despite aristocratic prejudices, the people are

virtuous by nature. A nation is really corrupted if, after having lost its character and its liberty, it changes from a democracy to an aristocracy or a monarchy; it is the death of the body politic by decay. Agis died in vain trying to recall the customs and laws of Lycurgus, which had been driven out of Sparta by avarice after a glorious four hundred year reign. No matter how much Demosthenes inveighed against Philip, the latter still found more eloquent advocates among the evil, degenerated Athenians. The population of Athens is still as numerous as in the times of Miltiades and Aristides, but there are no more Athenians. Who cares whether Brutus killed the tyrant? Tyranny still lives in men's hearts, and Rome lives only in Brutus.

We must stifle the domestic and foreign enemies of the Republic, or we will be destroyed with the Republic. Therefore, under the present circumstances, the most important part of your policy must be this: to influence the people by the use of reason, to influence the enemy of the people by the use of terror.

It has been said that terror is the means by which a despotic government rules. Is your rule similar to such a government? Yes, in the sense that the sword in the hands of the protector of liberty resembles the sword in the hands of the defender of tyranny. When a despot rules his stupefied subjects by means of terror he is justified as a despot. When you crush all the enemies of freedom by means of terror, you are justified as the founders of the Republic. The government of the revolution is the despotism of liberty against tyranny. Must force be used only in order to protect crime, and are thunderbolts not made to strike the heads of the proud?

Under the law of nature all physical and moral beings fight for their survival: crime strangles innocence so that it can rule, and innocence resists crime with all its strength. If tyranny rules but a single day, all the patriots will have been wiped out by the next morning. How long will the wrath of despots be considered just and the justice of the people be called cruel and rebellious? How kind people are to the oppressors and how unrelenting to the oppressed! Nothing is more natural; whoever doesn't hate crime cannot love virtue.

Yet either one or the other must succumb. "Be indulgent with the royalists!" some people shout; "have compassion for the criminal." No! Have compassion for innocence, for the weak, and for humanity!

Only the peaceful citizen has to be protected by society; in the republic, only republicans are citizens. The royalists and conspirators are foreigners to us or even enemies. Is not this terrible war in which liberty fights tyranny a single, indissoluble struggle? Are the enemies within not the allies of the enemies from without? . . . The intriguers who seek to purchase the conscience of the representatives of the people, the traitors who sell themselves, the mercenary pamphleteers who besmirch the cause of the people, who kill public virtue, who fan the fires of civil war and who are preparing for a political counter-revolution by means of a moral counter-revolution—are all these individuals any less dangerous than the tyrants whom they serve? . . .

To punish the oppressors of humanity is clemency; it would be barbarous to forgive them. The harshness of tyrants has only harshness as its basis: the harshness of republican governments stems from their benevolence. . . .

Give the French people this new pledge of your patriotic zeal, of your inexorable judgment of the guilty, and of your devotion to the people's cause. Let the principles of political ethics which we have just developed be proclaimed in your name both within and outside of the Republic.

CHATEAUBRIAND: *CHRISTIANITY AND PROGRESS*[4]

The July revolution of 1830 renewed the debate about the compatibility of the church and progressive democracy. Chateaubriand adopted a conciliatory position in the preface to his *Études Historiques* (1831).

✓   ✓   ✓

In this account I have stated how my ideas about Christianity differ from those of the Count de Maistre and of Father Lamennais: the former wants to reduce everyone to a common level of servitude, which is to be headed by a theocracy; the latter (if I am not mistaken) calls for general independence under the same theocratic domination. I demand the emancipation of mankind, just like my fellow-countryman, and just as he does, I demand man's emancipation from the clergy; I do not believe that the Pope should have any dictatorial powers of future republics. As I see it, in the Middle Ages Christianity became political by rigorous necessity: when nations lost their rights, religion, the only enlightened and powerful force left, had to take them over. Today people are resuming the exercise of these rights, and the Papacy naturally will have to give up these temporary functions and will have to abdicate its guardianship of the pupil now come of age. Resigning from politics, which it entered in the days of oppression and barbarism, the clergy will go back to the way of the primitive Church and limit itself to fighting false religions, false morality, and false philosophies. I believe that the political era of Christianity has ended; that its philosophical era is beginning; that the Papacy will be nothing more than the

[4] F. A. de Chateaubriand, *Études Historiques,* Paris: Furne, Jouvet et Cie, editeurs, 1872, pp. 73-74, 92-93.

pure source of all principles of faith, taking these in
their broadest and most rational sense. Catholic unity will
be personified in one venerable chief, the representative
of Christ on earth; as such he combines the truth of
God with the nature of man. Let the Sovereign Pontiff
always remain the guardian of these truths near the
relics of St. Peter and St. Paul. Let the people in a Christian Rome fall to their knees in front of an old man.
Would anything else be more suitable in the midst of so
many ruins? Could it offend our philosophy in any way?
The Pope is the only prince who blesses his subjects.

No truth is ever lost, therefore religious truth cannot
be destroyed; but it can be disfigured, abandoned, denied
by the sophistry and pride of those who no longer believe in the Son of God, by the ungrateful children of the
new synagogue. Moreover, I don't know of anything
more beautiful than an institution consecrated to these
truths, where souls can slake their thirst at the fountain
of life of which Isaiah spoke. The aversions of the
various sects for each other have disappeared; the children of Christ, no matter where their origin, crowd at
the foot of Mount Calvary, the natural founder of the
family. The disorder and the ambitions of the Roman
Court have ceased; at the Vatican only the virtue of the
first bishops, the protection of the arts, and majestic
memories remain. Everything tends to recompose Catholic unity; with a few concessions here and there an agreement was soon reached. I shall repeat once again:
Christianity waits for a superior genius, who will come
at this appointed time and place to renew its glory. The
Christian religion enters a new era; just like institutions
and customs, it too submits to a third transformation. It
ceases to be political and becomes philosophical, without, however, losing its divinity. Its circle widens with
increasing enlightenment and liberty, while the Cross remains its immovable center. . . .

Thus, from the foot of the Cross to the foot of Louis
XVI's scaffold, I bring together the three truths which
form the basis of social organization; religious truth,
philosophical truth or the independence of men's minds,
and political truth or liberty. I am trying to prove that
civilization is progressing, even if it seems to retrogress.

Man is moving towards an infinite perfection; he is still far from the sublime heights which all religious and primitive traditions tell us he once held, but he does not cease to climb the steep slope of this unknown Sinai, at the top of which he will find God. As society progresses it undergoes certain transformations, and we have reached one of those great changes in the human species.

The sons of Adam are all one family, moving towards the same goal. Events taking place in nations far removed from ours in time or space, which formerly hardly aroused our curiosity, now seem as important to us as though they were happening here, or had affected our own grandparents. Whole peoples were wiped out to preserve this liberty or that truth, this idea or that discovery for our benefit. Individuals were ready to suffer anything in order to add a talent of gold or even a farthing to the common wealth of humanity. In our turn, we shall bequeath any knowledge we may have gathered for the benefit of posterity. Over these constantly dying societies, new societies are forever being built; men fall by the wayside, but man remains standing, enriched by everything which his forefathers have transmitted, crowned by the lights and the gifts of all the ages, an ever growing giant, whose head touches the sky, and who will not stop until he reaches the Eternal throne.

Thus I am in agreement with the philosophy of my own century and with the modern school of history without abandoning the Christian truth. It is possible to differ with my opinions, but one has to admit that I did not bury my mind in the ruts of the past; I mapped out new routes: how happy I will be with the knowledge that I have been able to rectify a few historical and political errors.

— Reading No. 5 —

CHATEAUBRIAND: *SOCIAL ORDER AND PROGRESS*[5]

When he died in 1848 Chateaubriand left his famous *Mémoires d'outre Tombe* (*Recollections from Beyond the Tomb*). This work contains the following lines discussing the moral and social confusions possible in the age of transition from monarchy to democracy.

✓ ✓ ✓

Formerly, our eight centuries old monarchy in France was the center of European intelligence and the stronghold of European peace. Once deprived of this monarchy, Europe turned to democracy. For better or for worse, mankind has become its own master; the princes have been its guardian, but now that the nations have come of age they claim they no longer need a tutor. From the time of David down to the present day kingship has been a calling: now the rule of the people has started. In ancient times monarchy was the normal form of government throughout the world, even though there were a few exceptions like the small and short-lived republics of Greece, Carthage and Rome which all operated under a slave system. Since the banner of the French kings has ceased to fly, the whole of modern society has turned away from monarchy. In order to hasten the degradation of royal power in various countries, God has placed invalids or girls in their teens on the royal thrones. The sovereigns of this era of disbelief are lions without teeth, lionesses without nails, suckling babes or hardly affianced girls. . . .

Take note of the contradictions between the various

[5] Chateaubriand, *Mémoires d'outre Tombe, Edition du centenaire,* Paris: Flammarion, 1949, Second edition, Volume IV, Book XII, Conclusion: chapters 5 and 7, pp. 583-85, 592.

phenomena. Materially the world is improving, intellectual progress is being made, yet, instead of profiting from all this, the importance of nations has diminished. Why this contradiction?

The cause of all this is our moral degradation. Crimes have been committed at all times but never in cold blood as they are today, when we have lost our religious beliefs. Nowadays we no longer find crimes revolting; they are the result of a new age. If one did not always look at them in that way it is due to the fact that not much was known about the psychology of man. Today we analyze and probe into crimes as though they were a chemical ingredient, in order to find out how we can best utilize them. The corruption of the mind, which leads to much more destructiveness than the corruption of the senses, is taken for granted as a necessary result of all this. Corruption is no longer the monopoly of the perverse individual; it has become everyone's domain.

Modern man would be humiliated if he were told that he had a soul or that there is a life after death. He believes that if he does not raise himself above the pusillanimity of his fathers, he will lack steadfastness of purpose and strength of mind. He believes that nothingness, or if you prefer, doubt, is a truth that cannot be denied, even though it might be a disagreeable truth. Do admire our stupid pride!

This is how the contradiction between the withering away of society and the growth of the individual can be explained. If the increase in intelligence had brought about a corresponding growth of morality, a counterweight would have resulted, and humanity could have progressed without any danger. The very opposite has come about: as the light of intelligence has brightened, so the concept of right and wrong has become dimmed. Consciences have shrunk in proportion to the growth of ideas. Yes, society will perish. Liberty, which could have saved the world, will not be able to because it is not based on religion. Order and stability will be beaten by the anarchy of ideas. The purple, which used to symbolize power, will be the resting place of calamity; no one will be saved unless, like Christ, he is born in the manger. . . .

Now a few words about absolute equality: that equality would not only bring back the servitude of the body but also the enslavement of the mind; it would mean the destruction of the inequality of mind and body of the individual. Once our will is put under the supervision of the whole people, our abilities will atrophy from disuse. For example, the concept of infinity is one of man's attributes; once you forbid our minds and our emotions to concern themselves with unlimited good you have reduced human life to that of a snail, you have changed man into a machine. Don't let yourself be fooled about this, for without the possibility of achieving everything and without the concept of everlasting life, life would be completely empty. Without private property no one can be free; whoever does not own any property cannot be independent; he will remain a proletarian or a wage laborer, whether he lives in a capitalistic or in a communistic society. The common ownership of property will make all of society resemble one of those monasteries at whose door there always seemed to be a steward busily distributing bread. Hereditary and inviolable property are our personal safeguards; property is nothing but liberty. Absolute equality presupposes complete submission and would result in the harshest possible servitude. It would change man into a beast which must patiently submit to coercion and which walks forever along the beaten track. . . .

— Reading No. 6 —

DE MAISTRE: *WAR AND THE ETERNAL ORDER*[6]

The optimistic outlook of the eighteenth century and its confidence in man's power were rejected emphatically by the conservative reaction to the French Revolution. The most prominent spokesman for this reaction was the Count Joseph de Maistre who was ambassador to Saint Petersburg. In his *Les Soirées de Saint Pétersbourg* (*Evening Conversations in Saint Petersburg*) he advanced the following glorification and divine justification of war.

↗   ↗   ↗

The duties of the soldier are terrible, but they depend by necessity upon a major law of the universe. This alone can explain the fact that all the nations of the earth have agreed to see in this scourge something still more divine than all other scourges. Not without a great and profound reason does the title "Lord of Hosts" illumine every page of the Holy Scripture. Moreover, observe that this terrible law of war is nothing but a chapter of the general law governing the universe.

In Nature's vast domain an omnipresent violence reigns, a kind of ordained fury which arms all beings to mutual destruction. One can perceive this law even in the plant world, but as soon as one enters the animal world, the law becomes suddenly and horribly evident. There are insects of prey, reptiles of prey, birds of prey, fish of prey, and quadrupeds of prey. There is never a moment in which one living being is not devouring another. Above these numerous animal races stands man,

[6] *Les Soirées de Saint Petersbourg, ou Entretiens sur le Gouvernement Temporel de la Providence,* Fifth edition, Lyon: J. B. Pelagaud et Cie, 1845, Volume II, Seventh conversation, pp. 27-46.

whose destructive hand does not spare anything that lives. Man kills to eat, he kills to clothe himself, he kills to adorn himself, he kills to attack, he kills to defend himself, he kills to instruct himself, he kills to amuse himself, he kills for the sake of killing. A superb and terrible king, man needs everything and nothing resists him. . . .

The philosopher can even discover how the endless carnage is foreseen and ordained in the great overall plan. Should this law stop short of man? Certainly not. However, who should exterminate the one being that exterminates all the others? He himself. Man is commanded to strangle man. But how can he fulfill this law, he who is a moral and compassionate being, he who is born to love, he who weeps for others as he weeps for himself, who enjoys weeping and who finally invents fictions to make himself weep? War alone can fulfill this law.

Don't you hear the earth crying for blood? Neither the blood of animals nor of those guilty men executed by law satisfies it. If human justice would execute all who are guilty, there would be no war; but law reaches only a few and often spares even those, unaware that its ferocious humanitarianism contributes to the necessity of war. The earth does not cry in vain: war breaks out. Man is suddenly seized by the wild frenzy which differs from hatred or anger, and he advances to the field of battle without knowing what he wants or even what he does: what is the solution of this horrible enigma? Nothing is more contrary to his nature and yet nothing is less repugnant to him. He enthusiastically does what he abhors. Have you not observed that man never disobeys on the battlefield? I cannot recall a battlefield revolt, an agreement between forces to embrace and to reject the orders of a tyrant. Nothing resists, nothing can withstand the force which drives men into battle. Thus the great law of violent destruction of all living beings which starts with the flesh-worm and ends with man, fulfills itself. The earth, continually drenched in blood, is only an immense altar where everything that lives must be immolated endlessly, without respite, until all things are used up, the evil is extinguished, and death itself is dead. . . .

Thus war is in itself divine, because it is a law of the world. War is divine by its supernatural consequences. Who can doubt that death on the battlefield is a great privilege? Who can believe that the victims of this frightful judgment have shed their blood in vain? War is divine in the mysterious glory which surrounds it and in the equally inexplicable attraction which it exercises upon us . . .

War is divine by the manner in which it arises. I don't wish to condone anyone improperly, but how many of those who are regarded as the immediate instigators of wars are only carried away themselves by circumstances? At the precise moment effected by men and prescribed by justice, God advances to avenge the iniquities which the people of this earth have committed against Him. . . .

War is divine in its results which absolutely escape the speculations of human reason. Some wars debase nations for centuries, others exalt them, perfect them in various ways and, which is truly extraordinary, even replace the momentary losses by a visible increase in population. . . . War is divine also because of the indefinable force which determines successes. The famous saying "God is always with the big battalions" is true only in a limited sense. . . . An army of 40,000 men is physically inferior to an army of 60,000, but if the former has more courage, experience and discipline it can defeat the latter. . . . History is full of inconceivable events which baffle the most beautiful speculations. If you will glance at the rôle which moral forces play in a war, you will agree that nowhere does the Divine hand make itself felt to men more vividly. At no other time is man made more aware of his own nothingness and of the inevitable power which settles everything. . . . We must pray God not to send us fear. What man has never been afraid? Who has never had the occasion to wonder, in himself, around him, and in history, at the all powerful weakness of this passion, which often seems to control us at the very time when there is no reasonable motivation for it? Let's pray

God with all our strength to keep the fear which is at
His command, away from us and our friends; it is an
emotion which can ruin in one moment the most beautiful military speculations. . . . I believe wars are neither
won nor lost physically. This proposition contains nothing rigid; it offers itself to all its limitations, provided
that one agrees that the moral force has an immense
influence in war.

— Reading No. 7 —

DE MAISTRE: *ORDER AND JUSTICE*[7]

Can human reason understand, and therefore regulate,
the social order? Can man's judgment create a just order?
The Enlightenment and the French Revolution answered
with an emphatic yes. De Maistre, from his religious
point of view, countered with an equally emphatic no.

Let me propose the following argument. "God is unjust, cruel, without pity. God takes delight in the misfortunes of his creatures. Therefore . . ." and here I
hear the murmurers! "Therefore one should not pray."
On the contrary, nothing is more evident: Therefore one
must pray and must serve Him with much greater zeal
and anxiety than if His mercy were limitless as we imagine it. I wish to put a question. Suppose you lived under
the laws of a prince, I do not say an evil prince, but
only a severe and suspicious prince, who watches his
subjects closely. Would you take the same liberties with

[7] Count J. de Maistre, ibid., Eighth conversation, pp. 128-72.

him as with another and entirely different prince, who would be happy to know all his people free and who would ever fear to exercise his power lest he should be feared? Certainly not. Very well, the comparison is self-evident. The more terrible God appears to us, the more we must fear Him and the more our prayers must become ardent and indefatigable.

We know of God's existence with greater certainty than of His attributes; we know that He is before we know what He is; and we shall never fully know what He is. We find ourselves in a realm whose sovereign has proclaimed His laws once and forever. On the whole these laws seem wise and even kind; nevertheless some of them (I assume it for the moment) appear hard and even unjust. In this situation I ask all those who are dissatisfied, what should be done? Leave the realm, perhaps? Impossible: the realm is everywhere and nothing is without it. To complain, to sulk, to write against the sovereign? That would mean to be flogged or put to death. There is no better course than resignation and respect, I would even say love; for since we start with the supposition that the master exists and that we must serve Him absolutely, is it not better to serve Him, whatever His nature, with love than without it?

I do not wish to return to the argument of our preceding conversations by which we have refuted the complaints that some people dare to voice against Providence, but I wish to add that there is something intrinsically false and even foolish in these complaints, or, as the English say, a certain "nonsense" which is self-evident. What is the significance of complaints which are either sterile or sinful? They have no practical effect for man, and they don't help in any way to enlighten or perfect him. On the contrary, they can only harm him. They are useless to the atheist, and they are ridiculous and disastrous in the mouth of a theist. I cannot think of anything else as contrary to common sense.

But do you know whence comes this torrent of insolent doctrines which judge God without ceremony and ask him to account for his decrees? It comes from the large phalanx which is called "the intellectuals," a group whom we have not learned how to control in this century or to keep in their place—which is the second place. Formerly there were very few intellectuals, and only a fraction of these were impious. Today one sees nothing but intellectuals. They are a profession, a crowd, a whole people, and among them what was formerly an exception, which was bad enough, has become the rule. They have usurped a limitless influence from all sides. Yet if there is one thing certain in the world, it is, in my opinion, that it does not belong to science to lead men.

Nothing vital has been confided to science. One must have lost all sense to believe that God has charged the Academies with teaching us what He is and what we owe Him. The prelates, the noblemen, the high dignitaries of the state, are the true repositaries and guardians of the verities. It falls to them to teach the nations good and bad, truth and falsehood in the moral and spiritual order. Others have no right to reason about these things. The intellectuals have the natural sciences to amuse them: of what do they complain? Anybody who speaks or writes to deprive the people of a national dogma should be hanged as a thieving domestic. Rousseau himself has agreed to that without imagining the consequences for himself. Why have we been so imprudent as to allow everyone to speak freely? That is what has destroyed us. The intellectuals all have a certain ferocious and rebellious pride which does not accommodate itself to anything. They hate without exception all the distinctions which they do not enjoy themselves. Every authority displeases them. They hate everything that is above them. Let them, and they will attack everything, even God because He is the Lord. The same men have written against the kings and against Him who has established them.

SAINT-SIMON: *THE AGE OF INDUSTRY* [8]

Claude-Henri Comte de Saint-Simon was the first to foresee the implications of the industrial and scientific revolutions. "The Political Catechism of the Industrialists" predicted a new social and spiritual order based upon the ascendancy of the class of the real producers.

✓   ✓   ✓

Question. What is an industrialist?
Answer. Industrialists are men who work to produce something or who put various means of satisfying physical wants and tastes at society's disposal. . . . They form three great classes called farmers, manufacturers, and merchants.
Q. What rank should industrialists occupy in society?
A. The industrial class should occupy the first rank in society, for it is the most important class which is able to do without all the other classes. All other classes are the industrialist's creatures because their lives depend on his work, and in return all must work for him. In one word, because all is produced by industry all must center around it.
Q. What rank do the industrialists occupy in society?
A. In present-day society they are at the bottom of the social scale. Society gives more consideration to those who do work of secondary importance and even to the idle than to those who do the most important and the most useful work. . . .
Q. What do you want to accomplish by this catechism?
A. We will show the industrialists that their actual social position is on the lowest possible level and conse-

[8] Saint-Simon, *Oeuvres Complètes de Saint-Simon,* "*Catéchisme Politique des Industriels,*" Paris: Ad. Naquit, 1832, pp. 1-7, 12-13, 39, 44-48, 61-68, 206-09.

quently vastly inferior to the position they should hold
as the most capable and useful class in society. We will
trace the steps they must follow to attain the power and
the consideration now held by the first rank in society.
Q. Then, you are preaching insurrection and revolt in
this catechism? For the classes which are now invested
with power and consideration are certainly not disposed
to renounce their advantages voluntarily.
A. Far from preaching insurrection and revolt, we will
present the only possible means by which society can
escape from the violent acts which are sure to follow if
the industrial class remains passive in the midst of the
struggle for power. Public order and stability cannot be
maintained unless the most important industrialists are
in charge of public administration. The reason for that
is very simple: the general political tendency of the immense majority in society is to want a government which
governs little and cheaply, which is run by the most
capable men and in a manner which will assure complete public tranquillity. Hence, the only way in which
to satisfy these conditions and the will of the majority
is to put the most important industrialists in charge of
public administration, as they are the most interested in
maintaining public order, in practicing governmental
economy and in limiting arbitrary government. Finally,
of all members of society they have given the most positive proof of their administrative ability as is shown in
the success of their own enterprises. . . .
Q. Temporarily we admit that the industrialists will not
try to use violent methods to oust the bourgeoisie and
the nobility from their position as directors of public
finance and to replace them by the most important men
in their own class. But how will the industrialists bring
about this radical change in society of which we have
been speaking?
A. More than twenty-four twenty-fifths of the nation are
industrialists; therefore they have superior physical force.
They are the ones who produce all wealth; hence they
have financial power. They are superior in intelligence,
for it is they who devise and contribute most directly to
public prosperity. Finally, because they are the most
capable of administering the nation's finances, human

nature as well as divine nature charges the most important ones among them with the direction of finances. . . .

Q. There is one thing which you have not observed: there is an intermediate class between the nobles and the industrialists. That valuable class is the real social bond; it reconciles feudalist with industrialist principles. What do you think of this class?

A. The division which you have just established is metaphysically very beautiful. But we do not want to study metaphysical principles; on the contrary, we want to combat them. It is the aim of our work to put facts in the place of metaphysical reasoning. . . .

The jurists, the military commoners and the landed proprietors, who were neither members of the nobility nor peasants, composed this intermediary class. Usually they acted as protectors of the people against the pretensions and privileges of the nobility, the descendants of the Franks.

In 1789 the intermediate class felt strong enough to overthrow the supremacy of the descendants of the Franks and incited the masses to rebel against the nobles. The intermediate class then became the first class. It is very interesting to observe the behavior of this class after it came to power, for it reconstructed the feudal system for its own benefit.

This has been the conduct of the intermediate class which you have represented as being so useful to the industrialists. Of course, the middle class has rendered some services to the industrialists, but today the middle class, together with the nobility, bears down on the industrialists. . . . The industrialist class must . . . combine its own with the royal efforts to establish an industrial régime, that is to say a régime in which the most important industrialists will be at the top and will be in charge of administering the public wealth. . . .

A summary of the history of society has proven that the industrial class has continually grown in importance while other classes have lost importance. From this we conclude that the industrial class must in the end become more important than all the others.

Simple common sense has produced the following reasoning in the minds of men: people have always worked to better their lot, their goal has always been the establishment of a social order in which the class doing the most useful work will receive the greatest consideration, and it is this aim which society will finally fulfill.

Work is the source of all virtue; the most useful work is the most esteemed; thus human ethics and divine morality both place the industrialist class at the head of society. . . .

From Luther until this very day, the flow of ideas was mainly critical and revolutionary, it was a question of overthrowing the feudal government so that one would be able to work for the establishment of the social and industrial organization. But today, the industrial class being the strongest, the critical and revolutionary spirit must die out and a pacifist, organizational tendency must take its place.

In order to announce the formation of the pacifist and organizing party, we invite people seeking calm and stability to call themselves industrialists. This name indicates at the same time the goal and the means: the goal being the founding of social organization in the interest of the majority, the means being the entrusting of public finances to the most important industrialists.

However, the government may not, cannot and will not prevent the formation of the industrial party because this party is essentially pacifist and moral; because this party limits itself to influencing public opinion, and the government cannot prevent the formation of public opinion. . . .

Q. At least you must admit that it will take a long time before the industrialists will be educated to act according to their own interests.

A. We will need much less time than you imagine: one learns fast if it is to one's own interest to do so. The political education of the industrialist class will take much less time than you think; it will go much faster once the industrial system is publicized and capable men want to implement it; it is pleasant to swim with the current; it is so wasteful to work for the retrogression of civilization that once the concept of the industrial system is well established it must predominate. Then all skilled workers will stop trying to prolong the existence of feudal ruins in our political system.

The best trained men in science, in theology, in the fine arts, in law, in military science and in financial investment will soon join our venture. When this minority, trained in various skills, will work under the supervision of the foremost industrialists to establish this industrial system, the system will be promptly organized and quickly put to work. . . .

Obviously industrialism will give men the greatest possible general and individual liberty because it assures society of the best possible peace. It is equally evident that this régime will instill men with the highest type of morality while providing all of society with the greatest number of pleasures. . . .

Q. What are the advantages of the name "industrialism"?

A. The name "industrialism" emphasizes interests while liberalism only indicates sentiments. But interests are more important, for they are less variable than sentiments. Furthermore, the industrial class being the most numerous, any person who calls himself an industrialist professes his faith in that class, and states his intention of supporting the interest of the majority of the nation as against particular interests. . . .

SAINT-SIMON: *SOCIAL CHRISTIANITY*[9]

The last book which Count Saint-Simon wrote, *The New Christianity: Dialogue between a Conservative and a Reformer,* called for a synthesis of true Christianity and the age of industrialism.

✓   ✓   ✓

The Conservative. If the Christian religion is of divine origin, it cannot be perfected; yet by your writings you incite artists, industrialists and scientists to perfect this religion: thus you contradict yourself.

The Reformer. The contradiction between my opinion and my belief which you think you have detected is only an apparent one; you must distinguish between that which God has said personally and that which the clergy has said in His name. What God has said can certainly not be perfected, but what the clergy has said in God's name can be perfected like all other human knowledge. In certain epochs theology has to be renovated just like physics, chemistry or physiology.

C. What part of religion do you believe to be divine? What part do you believe to be human?

R. God has said: "Men must act as though they were each other's brothers." This sublime principle includes all that is divine in the Christian religion.

C. What! You reduce all the divine principles of Christianity to a single one?

R. God has necessarily related everything to this single principle; he has necessarily deduced everything from the same principle or he could not have drawn a systematic design for humanity. It would be blasphemous to

[9] Saint-Simon, *Nouveau Christianisme,* Paris: *au bureau du Globe,* 1832, pp. 9-11, 15-17, 20, 26, 69-70, 72-73, 82, 88-91.

pretend that the All-Powerful has based his religion on several principles.

Therefore, in accordance with the principle which God has given men as the law of conduct, they must organize society for the greatest good of the greatest number; the aim of all their work and all their action must be to better as quickly and as completely as possible the moral and material life of the most numerous class. I say that that, and only that, is the divine part of the Christian religion. . . .

C. What will become of the Christian religion if, as you believe, those men who teach it are heretics?

R. Christianity will be the only and the universal religion; the Asians and the Africans will be converted; members of the European clergy will again be good Christians, they will abandon the heresies which they profess nowadays. The true Christian doctrine, that is to say, the most general doctrine which can be deduced from the fundamental principle of divine morality, will come to the fore, and immediately thereafter all differences in religious opinion will disappear. . . .

It is the duty of Catholic clergymen, as well as of all other clergymen, to arouse in members of society the desire to do generally useful work. Thus, in their sermons and their personal conversations with the laity of their church, priests must use all their talents, as well as their intellects, to convince their audiences that improving the lot of the lowest class will also better that of the upper classes; for all are children in the eyes of God, the rich as well as the poor. In teaching children, as in the carrying out of all other parts of their belief and their doctrine, priests must demonstrate the following fact to their listeners: that the great majority of the population could easily enjoy a better life both materially and spiritually, and that the rich could better their own lives by increasing the happiness of the poor. . . .

Poets must support the work of the priests by writing poetry suitable to be recited at a religious service by all the members of the congregation, so that, all believers will be priests in each other's eyes. On their part musicians must also enrich religious poetry by composing music which will stir the souls of the believers. Painters and sculptors should call the Christian's attention in church to the most eminent deeds of good Christians. Architects must build the temples in such a way that the preachers, the poets and the musicians, the painters and the sculptors will all be able to arouse feelings of terror or joy and hope in the souls of the believers.

Here you see we have presented the foundations of religion and the means by which religious belief can be made useful to society. . . .

The new Christianity is called on to help the triumph of universal morality in its struggle with those principles which aim at the attainment of a particular good instead of the general good. This rejuvenated religion is called on to establish a permanent peace among all peoples by uniting them against any nation seeking its particular good at the expense of the general good, or against any government which may be anti-Christian enough to work for the good of the governors instead of that of the governed. This Christianity is called on to unite all men of learning, all artists and industrialists to make themselves general directors of humanity as well as directors of the special interests of the various peoples of the world. It is called on to place the fine arts, the sciences and industry at the head of sacred knowledge, while the Catholics have placed them among the profane fields of knowledge. Finally, this new Christianity is to declare all theology anathema and to classify all doctrines teaching man that there are other ways of attaining eternal life than by working with all one's strength for the betterment of one's fellow-man as impious. . . .

C. I have carefully followed your lecture; while you were talking my own ideas became clear, my doubts disappeared, and my love and admiration for the Christian religion increased. My ties with the religious system which has civilized Europe have not prevented me from understanding how it could be perfected, so that you have entirely converted me. . . .

What obstacles can lie in the path of your doctrine? Aren't those who would support it much more numerous than those who would obstruct it? The partisans of this doctrine base their action on the divine moral principle, while its adversaries found their actions on the

customs of ignorant and barbaric times, and on the egoistic principles of the Jesuits.

In brief, I believe that you should immediately propa-
gate your doctrine and set up missions in all civilized
countries which will work for its adoption.

R. The new Christians must develop the same character
and follow the same road as the primitive church; they
are only to use their intelligence to have their doctrine
adopted. They are to use nothing but persuasion and
demonstration to convert Catholics and Protestants. . . .
After having found the means of rejuvenating Christianity, my first care had to be to take all necessary precau-
tions to avoid any violence on the part of the poor
against the rich or the government as a consequence of
the spread of my new doctrine. First I had to address
myself to the rich and to the powerful to make them
favorably disposed towards my new doctrine, by showing them that the material and spiritual improvement of
the poorest class is not against their interests, since it
would increase their happiness as well. I had to show
the artists, the scientists and the chief industrialists that
their interests essentially correspond to those of the
masses, that they belong to the working class by being
its natural leaders, that the approbation of the masses is
the only reward worthy of their service and of their
wonderful work. . . .

— Reading No. 10 —

COMTE: *POSITIVIST RELIGION*[10]

Auguste Comte went further than his teacher Saint-Simon in developing a religion for the age of industrialism and positive science. He no longer spoke of new Christianity but of the Religion of Humanity.

✓   ✓   ✓

We come forward to deliver the Western world from an anarchical democracy and from a retrograde aristocracy. We come forward to constitute, as far as practicable, a real sociocracy; one which will be able to combine wisely, in furtherance of the common regeneration, all the powers of man, each of course brought to bear according to its own nature. In fact, we Sociocrats are as little democratical as we are aristocratical. In our eyes these two opposite parties—that is, their respectable portions—represent, though not in theory, on the one hand Solidarity, on the other, Continuity. These two ideas have hitherto been unfortunately antagonistic. Positivism removes this antagonism and replaces it with a subordination of the one to the other, by showing Solidarity to be subordinate to Continuity. So we adopt both these tendencies, in themselves and singly incomplete and incoherent; and we rise above them both equally. Yet at the present time we will by no means equally condemn the two parties which represent them. During the whole of my philosophical and social career, a period of thirty years, I have ever felt a profound contempt for that which, under our different governments, bore the name of the Opposition; I have felt a secret affinity for all constructive statesmen of whatever order. Even those who

[10] Auguste Comte, *Catechism of Positive Religion: Summary and Exposition of the Universal Religion,* tr. by Richard Congreve, London: John Chapman, 1858, from Preface and Conclusion, pp. 1-5, 11-14, 28-36, 407-28.

would build with evidently worn-out materials, I have never hesitated to prefer to the pure destructives in a century in which a general reconstruction is everywhere the chief want. Our official conservatives are behindhand, it is true. And yet, the mere revolutionist seems to me still more alien to the true spirit of the time; for in the middle of the nineteenth century, he blindly continues the negative line of action which could only suit the eighteenth. And he does not redeem the stagnation caused by his error, by the generous aspirations for a universal renovation, which were characteristic of his predecessors. . . .

Be this as it may, the retrograde nature of the worn-out ideas which our conservatives provisionally employ absolutely disqualifies them for directing political action in the midst of the present anarchy. For that anarchy has its origin in the irremediable weakness of the old beliefs. Western Europe no longer submits its reason to the guidance of opinions which evidently admit of no demonstrations, nay, which are radically illusory. For such is the character of all opinions of theological origin whatever the theology, be it even the purest Deism. All now recognize the fact that the practical activity of man must no longer waste itself on mutual hostilities, but must set itself peaceably to the resources of the earth—man's residence. Still less can we persist in the state of intellectual and moral childhood in which for the conduct of our life we look to motives which are absurd and degrading. The nineteenth century must never repeat the eighteenth, but neither must it break from it and reject it. It must continue the work of the eighteenth and realize at length the noble object of its wishes, a religion resting on demonstration, which directs the pacific activity of man. . . .

Positive religion gives full satisfaction to the intelligence of man and to his activity. Impelled onwards by the character of reality which distinguishes it, it has embraced the region of sentiment. We see no reason to fear that any thinkers worthy of the name, whether theoretical or practical, can commit the mistake made in the early period of Catholicism, and fail to see the superiority of a faith which is real and complete, which is social not by any accident, but by its own inherent nature. For the rest, it is for the nascent priesthood of Positivism and for all its true disciples, to secure, by their conduct as men and citizens, a due appreciation of its excellence. Even those who cannot be expected to form a judgment on its principles may be led by experience to a favorable conclusion. A doctrine which shall be seen to develop all human virtue—personal, domestic and civic —will soon gain the respect of all honest opponents, however strong may be their preference for an absolutist and egoistic rather than a relative and altruistic synthesis. . . .

My present work claims to furnish a systematic basis for the active propagation of Positivism. By so doing it necessarily forwards my principal construction, for it brings the new religion to bear on the classes which constitute its true social audience. The intellectual discipline instituted by Positive Philosophy rests on logical and scientific foundations of the utmost solidity; but no solidity can secure its prevalence, so antipathetic is its severe régime to minds trained as at present, unless it can gain the support of women and the proletarian class. That support should lend it irresistible strength. . . . The deep-seated intellectual anarchy of our time is another reason why Positive religion should appeal more particularly to the female sex. For that anarchy renders more necessary than ever the predominance of feeling, as it is feeling alone which preserves Western society from a complete and irreparable dissolution. Since the close of the Middle Ages, the influence of woman has been the sole though unacknowledged check on the moral evils naturally resulting from a state of mental alienation, the state which the West has been approximating more and more—and in the West, especially its centre —France. This chronic state of unreason is now at its height, and since no maxim of social experience can resist the corrosive effects of discussion as actually conducted, it is feeling alone that maintains order in the West. And even feeling is already seriously impaired. . . .

Four great classes constitute modern society. The four were destined to experience in succession the shock which the final regeneration of society rendered inevitable. The convulsion began in the last century with the intellectual element. The class which represented it rose in insurrection against the entire existing system based on the ideas of theology and war. The political explosion which was the natural result soon followed. It began with the middle classes who had long been eager to take the place of the nobility. Throughout Europe the nobility resisted, and its resistance could only be overcome by calling in the French proletariat to support their new political chiefs. Thus induced to mix in the great political struggle, the proletariat of Western Europe put forward its claim—a claim which there was no resisting because of its justice—to be incorporated into the system of modern society. It was advanced as soon as peace allowed the proletariat to make its wishes sufficiently clear. Still the revolutionary chain is incomplete, for it does not embrace the most fundamental element of the system of human order rightly viewed. The revolution, in regard to women, must be the complement of the revolution which enveloped the proletariat, just as this last, consolidating the revolution of the middle classes, sprung in its turn originally from the philosophical revolution. . . .

Woman's object is the same everywhere: to secure the due supremacy of moral force. She is led, therefore, to regard with especial reprobation all collective violence. She is still less ready to accept the yoke of numbers than that of wealth. Her influence will facilitate the industrial patriciate's advent to political power and that of the Positive priesthood; it will do this by leading both to unentangle themselves once and for all from the heterogeneous and ephemeral classes who headed the transition when it was in its negative phase. So completed, so purified, the revolution of Western Europe will proceed in a free and systematic course towards its peaceful termination, under the general direction of the true servants of Humanity. Their guidance will have an organic and progressive character which will completely reject all retrograde and anarchical parties. They will look upon anyone who persists in the theological or metaphysical state as disqualified by weakness of the brain for government. . . .

At the opening of the fourteenth century, then, begins the vast revolution in Western Europe, whose cessation is the mission of Positivism. The whole medieval régime was thoroughly broken up by conflicts between its component parts, while its doctrinal system remained intact. The chief struggle naturally was between the temporal and spiritual powers. This decisive revolution was completed in the fifteenth century when in every case, the national clergy became subordinate to the temporal authority. The Pope became a mere illusion as a spiritual centre; he sunk into the rôle of an Italian prince. With its independence, the priesthood lost its morality; first public, then private. To ensure its material existence, it placed its teaching at the service of the stronger authority. . . .

At the very commencement of the second phase of modern history, the negative doctrine directly broaches its anarchical principle, by its assertion of absolute individualism. This follows from its permit that everyone, with no conditions of competence exacted, may decide every question. Once this is allowed, all spiritual authority is at an end. The living rise in open insurrection against the dead, as is evidenced by the blind reprobation for the whole medieval system, for which the irrational admiration of antiquity was but a poor compensation. Protestantism lent its influence to widen the fatal breach in the continuity of the race which Catholicism had first opened. . . .

The anarchical character of its principles did not prevent Protestantism from aiding, at its commencement, the progress of science and the development of industry; for it gave a stimulus to individual effort, and it set aside oppressive rules. We owe two revolutions to it— that of Holland against the tyranny of Spain, and that of England to secure internal reform. The second was premature, and therefore ultimately failed. But it did not fail till it had given indications, under the admirable dictatorship of Cromwell, of the inevitable tendency of the European movement.

From this time forward the requirements of order and of progress, both equally imperative, became absolutely irreconcilable. The nations of Western Europe ranged themselves on one side or the other, according as they felt more strongly the need of order or of progress. . . .

It is easy then to understand the stormy character of the crisis, of the vast revolution which was the final issue of the whole five centuries which lie between us and the Middle Ages. That stormy character was the necessary result of the fatal inequality in the progression of the positive and negative movements. The two together make up the whole movement of Western Europe. The negative movement had been very rapid, and the positive had not been able to supply its demand for organization. The leadership in the work of modern regeneration, at the time of its greatest difficulty, had developed on the class least qualified for the post, the class of mere writers. The sole object of their aspirations was the pedantocracy dreamed of by their Greek masters. They would concentrate all power in their own persons. . . .

After a few years of hesitation under the Constituent Assembly, a decisive shock overthrew forever the retrograde institution of monarchy, last vestige of the caste system. The theocratic consecration given it by the servile clergy of modern times points to it as such. The glorious Convention, the only assembly that enjoys a real popularity in France, when it overthrew the monarchy as a preliminary step to social regeneration, had no power to supply any deficiencies in the intellectual movement of Western Europe. It lacked the requisites for a real organic policy. It was competent to direct in a heroic manner the defence of the French Republic, but it could not do more than express in vague form the program of social wants; and even this was obscured by a metaphysical philosophy which has always been incapable of any constructiveness whatever.

The political triumph of the negative doctrine brought its thoroughly subversive tendencies to light. This soon led to a retrograde reaction. The reaction began under the ephemeral ascendancy of a bloodthirsty Deism in the person of Robespierre. The reaction grew in the official restoration of Catholicism under the military tyranny of Buonaparte. But the primary tendencies of modern civilization reject alike theology and war. Though every

egoistic instinct was stimulated at that time to an un-
paralleled extent, the military spirit was yet obliged in
its last orgies, to rest on a system of compulsory recruit-
ment. The universal adoption of conscription is a sign
that the abolition of standing armies is approaching.
Their substitute will be a police force. The expedients
to which a retrograde policy has since been driven to
avert such a result have all failed; it has been found as
impossible to revive a warlike spirit as a theological one.
The expedition to Algiers was the most immoral of these
expedients; and I venture in this place, in the name of
true Positivists, solemnly to proclaim my wish that the
Arabs may forcibly expel the French, unless the French
consent to an act of noble restitution.

The retrograde movement under the first Napoleon
drew its apparent strength solely from war. The extent
of its failure was evident on the final restoration of
peace. In the absence, however, of all organic views, the
spiritual anarchy reached its height. All the previous convictions of men, whether of the revolutionary or retrograde school, lost their hold. If discipline is partial it
cannot be real and lasting. If it is to be universal, it
must rest on one principle—the constant supremacy of
the heart over the intellect. But the principle had been
losing ground ever since the close of the Middle Ages.
It had the support of women, but this holy support was
powerless; for Western Europe, in its madness, paid less
and less respect to women. The result was that even in
the scientific sphere, the provisional order which Bacon
and Descartes had tried to institute, was set aside; and
free course was given on empirical grounds to the un-
connected study of special sciences. All philosophical
control was scorned by those who engaged in such pur-
suits. Every effort was made to give each science an
indefinite extension by isolating it from the whole. At
each step in this process the whole was lost sight of
more completely. The movement became retrograde as
well as anarchical, for it threatened to destroy even the
great results of former labors while it gave increased
power to academic mediocrity. In the domain of art we
find anarchy and retrogression still more rampant. Art
is by its nature eminently synthetic; it rejects analytic

empiricism more absolutely than science does. Yet even in poetry the degradation was so great that the learned could appreciate nothing but style. This was carried to such an extent that they often placed real masterpieces below compositions which were both poor and immoral. . . .

. . . The result of the whole positive movement was to facilitate the advent of sociology—a birth which had been heralded by Condorcet in his attempt to bring the future into systematic subordination to the past. His attempt failed, but it is nonetheless immortal. It was made at a time when men's minds were in a state most entirely averse to all sound historical conceptions.

By the universal adoption of an exclusively human point of view, it was possible for a subjective synthesis to construct a philosophy which should be proof against all objections. The next step after the synthesis was to found the final religion. To this I was led as soon as the renovation of the intellect had been followed by a regeneration of the moral nature. . . .

All noble hearts and all great intellects may converge for the future. They accept this termination of the long and difficult initiation through which Humanity has had to pass, under the sway of powers which have been constantly on the decline—theology and war. . . . The relative finally takes the place of the absolute; altruism tends to control egoism; systematic progress is substituted for spontaneous growth. In a word, Humanity definitively occupies the place of God, but she does not forget the services which the idea of God provisionally rendered. . . .

LOUIS NAPOLEON: *NAPOLEONIC IDEAS*[11]

In 1839 Napoléon-Louis Bonaparte, then living in exile in England as a pretender to the French imperial throne, published his *Des Idées Napoléoniennes*. In this work the future Napoleon III praised his uncle's reign as the ideal régime for France and the European continent.

ᛐ   ᛐ   ᛐ

The Emperor Napoleon has contributed more than any other person to hasten the reign of liberty, by preserving the moral influence of the revolution, and diminishing the fears which it inspired. Without the Consulate and the Empire, the revolution would have been merely a great drama, leaving grand recollections, but few practical results. The revolution would have been drowned in the counter-revolution; but the contrary took place, because Napoleon planted deep in France, and introduced everywhere in Europe, the principal benefits resulting from the grand crisis of 1789, and because, to use his language, "he purified the revolution, seated firmly kings, and ennobled the people." He purified the revolution, by separating the truths, which it caused to triumph, from the passions, which, in their delirium, had obscured them; he seated firmly kings, by rendering royal power respectable and honorable; he ennobled the people, by giving them a consciousness of their strength, and those institutions which elevate man in his own respect. The Emperor should be regarded as the Messiah of new ideas; for, in moments which immediately follow a social dissolution, the essential thing is, not to

[11] Napoléon-Louis Bonaparte, *Napoleonic Ideas,* tr. by James A. Dorr, New York: Appleton & Co., 1859, pp. 25-27, 35-36, 88-90, 136-43, 149-54.

put into application principles in all the subtility of their theory, but to seize the regenerating spirit, to identify one's self with the sentiments of the people, and guide them boldly towards the end which they desire to reach. To be capable of accomplishing such a task, it is necessary that "your fibre should respond to that of the people," that you feel as the people feel, and that your interests be so intermingled, that you must conquer or fall together! . . .

The Emperor acquired so easily his immense ascendency, because he was the representative of the true ideas of his age. As to harmful ideas, he never attacked them in front, but always in flank, parleying and negotiating with them, and finally reducing them to submission by a moral influence; for he knew that violence is unavailing and worthless against ideas.

Having always an object in view, he employed, according to circumstances, the most prompt means to attain it. What was his ultimate object? . . . Liberty. . . .

The predominant idea, which presided over all the internal establishments of the Emperor, was the desire to found civil order. France was surrounded by powerful neighbors. Since Henry IV, she had been the object of the jealousy of Europe. She required a large permanent army to maintain her independence. That army was organized; it had its colonels, its generals, its marshals; but the rest of the nation was not organized; and by the side of this military hierarchy, by the side of these dignities to which glory lent so much lustre, it was necessary that there should be civil dignities of equal weight and influence; otherwise the government would always be in danger of falling into the hands of a fortunate soldier. The United States offer us a striking example of the inconveniences, which attend the weakness of a civil authority. Although, in that country, there are none of the fermentations of discord, which for a long time yet will trouble Europe, the central power, being weak, is alarmed at every independent organization; for every independent organization threatens it. It is not military power alone which is feared; but money power—the bank: hence a division of parties. The president of the bank might have more power than the President of the country; for a much stronger reason, a successful general would soon eclipse the civil power. In the Italian republics, as in England, the aristocracy constituted the organized civil order; but France having, happily, no longer any privileged bodies, it was by means of a democratic hierarchy, which should not offend the principle of equality, that the same advantages were to be secured. . . .

Napoleon was the supreme chief of the state, the elect of the people, the representative of the nation. In his public acts, it was the Emperor's pride to acknowledge that he owed everything to the French people. When at the foot of the Pyrenees, surrounded by kings and the object of their homage, he disposed of thrones and empires, he claimed with energy the title of first representative of the people, a title which seemed about to be given exclusively to members of the legislative body. . . .

When the fortune of arms had rendered Napoleon master of the greater part of the continent, he desired to use his conquests for the establishment of a European confederation.

Prompt to apprehend the tendency of civilization, the Emperor hastened its march by executing, without delay, that which otherwise had been enfolded in the distant decrees of Providence. His genius foresaw that the rivalry which separates the different nations of Europe would disappear before a general interest well understood. . . .

To replace among the nations of Europe the state of nature by the social state,—such was the idea of the Emperor; all his political combinations tended to this great end; but it was necessary, in order to reach it, to bring England and Russia to a frank concurrence in his views. . . .

The policy of the Emperor, . . . consisted in founding a solid European association, by causing his system to rest upon complete nationalities, and upon general interests fairly satisfied. . . . In order to cement the European association, the Emperor, to use his own words, would have caused to be adopted a European code, and a European court of cassation, to correct all errors, as the Court of Cassation in France corrects the errors of

French tribunals. He would have founded a European Institute to animate, direct, and unite all the learned associations of Europe. Uniformity of coins and money, weights and measures, and uniformity in legislation, would have been secured by his powerful intervention. . . .

The government of Napoleon, better than any other, could have sustained liberty, for the simple reason that liberty would have strengthened his throne, though it overthrows such thrones as have not a solid foundation.

Liberty would have fortified his power, because Napoleon had established in France all that ought to precede liberty; because his power reposed upon the whole mass of the nation; because his interests were the same as those of the people; because, finally, the most perfect confidence reigned between the ruler and the governed. . . .

Beloved especially by the people, could Napoleon fear to grant political rights to all the citizens? After being chosen consul for life, he re-established the principle of the right of election, and used these significant words: "For the sake of the stability of the government, it is necessary that the people should have a share in the elections!" Thus already in 1803, Napoleon foresaw that liberty would fortify his power. His warmest partisans being among the people, the more he lowered the electoral qualification, the better chances had his natural friends of arriving at the legislative assembly; the more power he gave to the masses, the more he strengthened his own.

Nor would liberty of discussion in the Chambers have endangered the imperial government; for, all being agreed upon the fundamental questions, an opposition would only have had the effect of giving birth to a noble emulation, and instead of expending its energies in attempting the overthrow of government, it would have confined its efforts to endeavoring to improve it. . . .

Napoleon's plans were constantly enlarged in proportion with the elements which he had at his disposition, and he fell because he desired to accomplish in ten years a work which would have required several generations.

Not then in consequence of impotence did the Emperor succumb, but in consequence of exhaustion. And in spite of his terrible reverses, innumerable calamities, the French people always supported him by their suffrages, sustained him by their efforts, and encouraged him by their attachment. . . .

The period of the Empire was a war of life and death, waged by England against France. England triumphed; but, thanks to the creative genius of Napoleon, France, although vanquished, has lost, substantially, less than England. The finances of France are still the most prosperous in Europe; England bends under the weight of debt. The impulse given to industry and to commerce has not been stopped in spite of our reverses; and at this time the European continent supplies itself with the greater part of the products which England formerly supplied.

Now, we ask, who are the greatest statesmen, those who have ruled over countries which have gained, in spite of defeat, or those who have governed countries which have lost, in spite of victory? . . .

Let us then ask again, who are the greatest statesmen, those who found a system which crumbles in spite of their all-sufficient power, or those who found a system which survives their defeat, and rises from its ruins?

The Napoleonic Ideas have then the character of ideas which control the movement of society, since they advance by their own force, although deprived of their author; like a body which, launched into space, arrives by its own momentum and weight at the end designed.

There is no longer any necessity to reconstruct the system of the Emperor; it will reconstruct itself. Sovereigns and nations will concur in re-establishing it; because each one will see in it a guaranty of order, of peace, and of prosperity. . . .

In conclusion, let us repeat it, the Napoleonic Idea is not one of war, but a social, industrial, commercial idea, and one which concerns all mankind. If to some it appears always surrounded by the thunder of combats, that is because it was in fact for too long a time veiled by the smoke of cannon and the dust of battles. But now the clouds are dispersed, and we can see, beyond the glory of arms, a civil glory greater and more enduring. . . .

— Reading No. 12 —

MICHELET: *THE HERITAGE OF THE REVOLUTION* [12]

In his monumental *History of the French Revolution* Jules Michelet combined an intense nationalism with democratic radicalism. No other historian has so vividly presented the dominant rôle which the Revolution continues to play in all the cultural and political issues dividing French society.

✓   ✓   ✓

The Revolution lives in ourselves,—in our souls; it has no outward monument. Living spirit of France, where shall I seize thee, but within myself?—The governments that have succeeded each other, hostile in all other respects, appear at least agreed in this, to resuscitate, to awaken remote and departed ages. But thee they would have wished to bury. Yet why? Thou, thou alone dost live. . . .

Alas! poor Revolution. How confidingly on thy first day didst thou invite the world to love and peace. "O

[12] Michelet, *Historical View of the French Revolution, from Its Earliest Indications to the Flight of the King in 1791,* tr. by C. Cocks, New ed., London: S. Bell & Sons, 1890, Preface, Book III (The New Religion), Book IV (The Struggle of Principles and the First Step of Terror).

my enemies," didst thou exclaim, "there are no longer any enemies." Thou didst stretch forth thy hand to all and offer them thy cup to drink to the peace of nations — But they would not.

And even when they advanced to inflict a treacherous wound, the sword drawn by France was the sword of peace. It was to deliver the nations and give them true peace—liberty, that she struck the tyrants. Dante asserts Eternal Love to be the founder of the gates of hell. And thus the Revolution wrote Peace upon her flag of war. . . .

France had so completely identified herself with this thought that she did her utmost to restrain herself from achieving conquests. Every nation needing the same blessing—liberty—and pursuing the same right, whence could war possibly arise? Could the Revolution, which, in its principle, was but the triumph of right, the resurrection of justice, the tardy reaction of thought against brute force,—could it, without provocation, have recourse to violence?

This utterly pacific, benevolent, loving character of the Revolution seems today a paradox:—so unknown is its origin, so misunderstood its nature, and so obscured its tradition, in so short a time!

The violent, terrible efforts which it was obliged to make in order not to perish in a struggle with the conspiring world, has been mistaken for the Revolution itself by a blind, forgetful generation.

And from this confusion has resulted a serious, deeply rooted evil, very difficult to be cured among the French people; the adoration of force: The force of resistance, the desperate effort to defend unity, '93. They shudder and fall on their knees. The force of invasion and conquest, 1800; the Alps brought low and the thunder of Austerlitz. They fall prostrate and adore.

Shall I add that in 1815, with too great a tendency to overvalue force and to mistake success for a judgment of God, the French found at the bottom of their hearts, in their grief and anger, a miserable argument for justifying their enemy. Many whispered to themselves, "they are strong, therefore they are just."

Thus, two evils, the greatest that can afflict a people,

fell upon France at once. Her own tradition slipped away from her, she forgot herself. And, every day more uncertain, paler, and more fleeting, the doubtful image of Right flitted before her eyes. Let us not take the trouble to inquire why this nation continues to sink gradually lower and becomes weaker. Attribute not its decline to outward causes; let it not accuse either heaven or earth; the evil is in itself.

The reason why an insidious tyranny was able to render it a prey to corruption is that it was itself corruptible. Like a wretched man deprived of sight, it groped its way in a miry road: it no longer saw its star. What! the star of victory? No, the sum of Justice and of the Revolution. . . .

Nothing was more fatal to the Revolution than to be self-ignorant in a religious point of view,—not to know that it was a religion in itself.

It neither knew itself nor Christianity; it knew not exactly whether it was conformable or contrary to Christianity—whether it was to go back to it or to march forward.

In its easy confidence, it welcomed with pleasure the sympathy testified towards it by the bulk of the lower clergy. It was told, and it expected that it was about to realize the promises of the Gospel; that it was called to reform and renew Christianity, and not to replace it. It believed this and marched in this direction; but, at its second step, it found that the priests had become priests again, the enemies of the Revolution; and the Church appeared what it really was—the obstacle, the main impediment, far more even than royalty. . . .

The Jacobins, by their party spirit, by their fervent and relentless faith, and by their keen and searching inquisitiveness, partook somewhat of the character of the priest. They formed, so to speak, a revolutionary clergy, of which Robespierre became gradually the chief. . . .

Robespierre used to say, in speaking of the Cordelier Camille Desmoulins (therefore, with greater reason, of the other Cordeliers still more impetuous): "They are going too fast; they will break their necks; Paris was not made in a day, and it requires more than a day to un-make it."

The audacity and the grand initiative of the Revolution belonged to the club of the Cordeliers. Almost opposite the *École de Medecine,* you will perceive, at the bottom of a court-yard, a chapel of a plain but solid style of architecture. This is the sibylline den of the Revolution, the Club of the Cordeliers. There was her frenzy, her tripod, and her oracle. . . .

How strange was the fatality of this place! This edifice had belonged to the Revolution ever since the thirteenth century, and always to its most eccentric genius. There is not as much difference as might be supposed between those Cordelier friars and these Cordelier republicans, or between Mendicant friars and the Sans-Culottes. Religious disputation and political disputation, the school of the Middle Ages and the club of 1790, differ rather in form than in spirit. . . .

The faith of the ancient Cordeliers, eminently revolutionary, was the inspiration of illumination of the simple and poor. They made poverty the first Christian virtue and carried its ambition to an incredible degree, even to the acceptance of death by burning rather than any change in their Mendicant robe. True Sans-Culottes of the Middle Ages in their animosity against property, they went beyond their successors of the Club of the Cordeliers and the whole revolution, not excepting Babeuf.

Our revolutionary Cordeliers have, like those of the Middle Ages, an absolute faith in the instinct of the simple; only, instead of divine light, they term it popular reason. Their genius, entirely instinctive and spontaneous, now inspired, now infuriated, distinguishes them profoundly from the calculating enthusiasm and the moody cold fanaticism which characterizes the Jacobins. . . .

Marat, furious and blind as he was, seems to have perceived the danger of this anarchical spirit; and he proposed very early the dictatorship of a military tribune, and later the creation of three State Inquisitors. He seemed to envy the organization of the Jacobin Society; and in December, 1790, he proposed to institute, doubtless on the plan of that Society, a brotherhood of spiers and informers to watch and denounce the agents of the government. This idea was not carried out, and Marat alone became his own inquisition. Information and complaints, just or unjust, founded or unfounded, were forwarded to him from every side; and he believed them all and printed them all. . . .

The violent, sudden transition from a life of study to revolutionary commotion, had attacked his brain and made him like a drunken man. The counterfeiters and imitators of his paper, who, assuming his name and title, forged upon him their own opinions, contributed not a little to the increase of his fury. He would trust to nobody for prosecuting them, but would go himself in pursuit of their hawkers, watching for them at the corners of the streets, and sometimes catching them at night. The police, on its side, was in search of Marat, to arrest him; and he was obliged to fly wherever he could. His poor and wretched manner of living and his forced retirement rendered him the more nervous and irritable. In the violent paroxysms of his indignation and his compassion for the people, he relieved his furious sensitivity by atrocious accusations, wishes for massacres, and counsels for assassination. His distrust ever increasing, the number of the guilty and of the necessary victims likewise increasing in his mind, this Friend of the People would in time have exterminated the people.

The year 1791, so sadly commenced by the scene of the 4th of January, presents from the very first the appearance of a fatal change, trampling upon the rights of liberty,—an appeal to force. . . .

What, in my opinion, does Marat greater wrong than all his furious language, is that he is not so much a madman or a monomaniac, but he remembers his personal enemies wonderfully well. If he wished to merit the grand name of Friend of the People and render sacred the terrible character of national accuser that he had assumed, it was necessary first to be pure and disinterested. To be so from money is not sufficient; it is necessary to be also pure from hatred. . . .

In the extremely critical position in which France was then, being neither at peace nor at war, and having in her heart that hostile royalty, that immense conspiracy of priests and nobles, and the public authority being precisely in the hands of those against whom it was to be directed, what power remained for France? No other, it would seem at first glance, than popular intimidation. But this intimidation had a dreadful result: by paralyzing the hostile power and removing the present momentary obstacle, it would go on forever creating an obstacle which would increase and necessitate the employment of a new degree of Terror.

The Jacobins seem to conduct themselves as the immediate heirs of the priests: they imitate the vexatious intolerance by which the clergy has occasioned so many heresies; and they boldly follow the old dogma: "Outside our community, no salvation." Excepting the Cordeliers, whom they treat gently, speaking of them as little as possible, they persecute the clubs, even those of a revolutionary character.

This agitation, serious in itself, has been far more so inasmuch as it was a field of battle where two principles and two spirits met and struggled: one, the original and natural principle which had produced the Revolution, namely, justice and equitable humanity,—and the other, the principle of expedients and interest, which was called public safety, and which ruined France. It ruined her, casting her into a crescendo of assassination which could not be stopped; it made France execrable throughout Europe and inspired everlasting hatred against her. It ruined her because the minds of men, being dejected after the Reign of Terror, from disgust and remorse, rushed blindly to the yoke of military despotism; it ruined her because this glorious tyranny ended in placing her enemies in Paris, and her chief at Saint Helena.

Ten years of public safety by the hand of the republicans, and fifteen years of public safety by the sword of the emperor . . . Open the book of the debt, you are still paying at the present day for the ransom of France. The territory was redeemed; but the souls of men still remain unredeemed. I see them still serfs, the slaves of cupidity and base passions, preserving of this sanguinary history only the adoration of strength and victory,—of strength that was weak, and of victory vanquished.

What has not been vanquished, is the principle of the

Revolution, disinterested justice, equity in spite of everything, and to this we must return.

— Reading No. 13 —

TOCQUEVILLE: *THE FUTURE OF LIBERTY*[13]

Alexis Count de Tocqueville wrote numerous letters in which he often expressed his political ideas more clearly than in his two great books. De Tocqueville was an adherent of liberty, but he saw the danger of a new despotism and witnessed its rise under Napoleon III.

⁄ *⁄* *⁄*

My critics insist upon making me out a party-man; but I am not that. Passions are attributed to me where I have only opinions; but rather, I have but one opinion, an enthusiasm for liberty and for the dignity of the human race. I consider all forms of government merely as so many more or less perfect means of satisfying this holy and legitimate craving. People ascribe to me alternately aristocratic and democratic prejudices. If I had been born in another period or in another country, I might have had either one or the other. But my birth as

[13] Letters to Henry Reeve (1813-1895), March 22, 1837; to Pierre Paul Royer-Collard (1786-1845), April 4, 1838; to the *Times*, London, December 11, 1851; to Camille Odilon Barrot (1791-1873), October 26, 1873. See Tocqueville, *Nouvelles Correspondences entièrement inédites*, Paris: Levy, 1866, pp. 163-66, 300-02, and *Oeuvres et Correspondance inédites*, pp. 69-70.

it happened, made it easy for me to guard against both. I came into the world at the end of a long revolution, which, after destroying ancient institutions, created none that could last. When I entered life, aristocracy was dead and democracy was yet unborn. My instinct, therefore, could not lead me blindly either to the one or the other. I lived in a country which for forty years had tried everything and settled nothing. I was on my guard, therefore, against political illusions. Belonging myself to the ancient aristocracy of my country, I had no natural hatred or jealousy of the aristocracy, nor could I have any natural affection for it, since that aristocracy had ceased to exist, and one can be strongly attached only to the living. I was near enough to know it thoroughly, and far enough to judge it dispassionately. I may say as much for the democratic element. It had done me, as an individual, neither good nor evil. I had no personal motive, apart from my public convictions, to love or hate it. Balanced between the past and the future, with no natural instinctive attraction towards either, I could, without an effort, quietly contemplate each side of the question.

I shall speak little to you of the political situation which is not fully clear to me, my heart being too occupied elsewhere to stick to it in any case. I shall surprise you perhaps by saying that among so many bills which have piled up on the desk of the Chamber, there is only one which really interests me and which seems to me to have a strong bearing on the future, and this is the bill dealing with firms in partnership. The world is turning to industry because industry leads to comfort. It seems to me that no matter what—industrial interests are going to become the strongest of all. In a century such as ours, to entrust the direction of industry to the discretion of the government, means to put in its hands once more an immense power which the future will continually augment; it means to entrust it with the control over that which, in my opinion, will become the strongest and most intimate concern of the human heart; or rather, it means to give it the heart itself of future generations. . . . The government's scheme can do some good for the moment, but it may bring about lasting harm: it highly strengthens the long chain which already envelops and closes in on all sides of individual existence.

The liberty of the press is destroyed to an extent unheard of even in the time of the empire. . . . Human life is as little respeced as human liberty. . . . As for the appeal to the people, to which Louis Napoleon affects to submit his claims, never was a more odious mockery offered to a nation . . . The people is called upon to express its opinion; but the first measure taken to obtain it is to establish military terrorism throughout the country . . . ; such . . . is the condition in which we stand. Force overturning law, trampling on the liberty of the press and of the person, deriding the popular will, in whose name the Government pretends to act—France torn from the alliance of free nations to be yoked to the despotic monarchies of the Continent—such is the result of the coup d'état. If the judgment of the people of England can approve these military saturnalia, and if the facts I have related and to which I pledge accurate truth, do not rouse its censures: I shall mourn for you and for ourselves and for the sacred cause of legal liberty throughout the world; for the public opinion of England is the grand jury of mankind in the cause of freedom, and if its verdict were to acquit the oppressor, the oppressed would have no other recourse but in God . . .

Both of us belong to another age. We are a type of antediluvian animals that soon will have to be put in museums of natural history, to know how in times past, beings were so oddly made as to love liberty, law, sincerity: strange tastes which demand organs absolutely different from those with which the inhabitants of the present world are provided. I am convinced that the present race will pass and will be replaced by another with greater similarity to us than it. But shall we see this new transformation? I doubt it. It will take a long time . . . for Frenchmen to return, I do not say to the passionate desire for liberty, but to that pride in themselves, to that habit of speaking and writing freely, the need for at least discussing their subjection, which is in the spirit of the century and in the oldest instinct of their race. When I think of the trials which a handful of political adventurers have caused this unhappy country to undergo; when I think that in the heart of this rich and industrious society, one has reached the point of even putting into jeopardy the right of property, when I recall these things and think, that in truth the human species is composed for the most part of weak, honest and common souls, I am tempted to excuse this terrific moral let-down which we are witnessing, and to reserve all my ire and scorn for the intriguers and mad ones who have thrown our country into such dire straits.

— Reading No. 14 —

TOCQUEVILLE: *FRENCH FOREIGN POLICY* 14

During the Crimean War (1854-1856), France, as England's ally, fought against Russia. Tocqueville wrote about European policy and Europe's future to English friends, discussing France's relationship to England and Russia.

✓   ✓   ✓

I shall venture only a few words in reply to what you write concerning the alliance of our two nations. I do

14 Letters to William Rathbone Greg (1809-1881), April 26, 1854; and to Nassau William Senior (1790-1854), Feb. 15 and Sept. 19, 1855. See *Nouvelles Correspondences, op. cit., pp. 325 27, 365 67, 371 76.*

not have to tell you that I view this alliance with pleasure; I have always believed it the most desirable event which could take place. It alone can assure not only the general liberties of Europe, as you put it, but the prospect of the individual liberties of the European peoples. For Russia is the cornerstone of despotism in the world, and were this stone torn from the hands of the despots, it would sooner or later lead to the fall of all absolute governments. Hence, I hope with all my heart, both as a European and as a Frenchman, that the alliance will last and will be successful. As for the realization of this wish, it is constantly in my mind. The French people are most assuredly inclined, on the whole, not only to live in peace with England but to be on the closest terms with her. The daily intercourse which has existed between these two peoples for the last forty years has gone far to eliminate old hates and to destroy old prejudices. But you are not unaware that, today, it is less a question of the inclinations of the nation than of one man; and no one has ever known precisely what goes on in his mind.

According to many continental notions, a nation which cannot raise as many troops as its wants require loses our respect. It ceases, according to our notions, to be great or even patriotic. . . . Considering how difficult it is to procure soldiers by voluntary enlistment, . . . I do not see how you will be able to hold your high rank, unless your people will consent to something resembling military conscription.

In general, dangerous as it is to speak of a foreign country, I venture to say that England is mistaken if she thinks that she can continue separated from the rest of the world and preserve all her peculiar institutions uninfluenced by those which prevail over the whole of the Continent.

In the period in which we live, and still more, in the period which is approaching, no European nation can long remain absolutely dissimilar to all others. I believe that a law existing over the whole continent must in time influence the laws of Great Britain, notwithstanding the sea, and notwithstanding the habits and institutions which, still more than the sea, have separated you from us, up to the present time.

My prophecies may not be fulfilled in our time; but I should not be sorry to deposit this letter with a notary, to be opened and their truth or falsehood proved, fifty years hence.

About a month ago I read some remarkable articles in the German papers, which you perhaps have seen, on the progress which Russia is making in the Far East. The writer seems to be a man of sense and well informed.

It appears that during the last five years, Russia, profiting by the Chinese disturbances, has seized not only the mouth of the Amur but a large territory in Mongolia, and has also gained a considerable portion of the tribes which inhabit it. You know that these tribes once overran all Asia and have twice conquered China. The means have always been the same: some accident which, for an instant, has united these tribes in submission to the will of one man. Now, says the writer very plausibly, the Tsar may bring this about, and do what has been done by Genghis Khan, and indeed by others.

If these designs are carried out, all Upper Asia will be at the mercy of a man who, though the seat of his power is in Europe, can unite the Mongols.

RENAN: *DEMOCRACY IN FRANCE*[15]

Ernest Renan was a scholar and an intellectual aristocrat. In the preface to his *Recollections of My Youth,* Renan attempted to define the position of the intellectuals and of scholarship in a democratic France.

✓ ✓ ✓

We must not, because of our personal tastes, our prejudices perhaps, set ourselves to oppose the action of our time. This action goes on without regard to us, and probably it is right. The world is moving in the direction of what I may call a kind of Americanism, which shocks our refined ideas, but which, once the crisis of the present hour is over, may very possibly be less inimical than the *ancien régime* to the only thing of any real importance; viz. the emancipation and progress of the human mind. . . . The one object in life is the development of the mind, and the first condition for the development of the mind is that it should have liberty. The worst social state from this point of view is the theocratic state, like Islam or the ancient Pontifical state, in which dogma reigns supreme. Nations with an exclusive state religion, like Spain, are not much better off. Nations in which a religion of the majority is recognized are also exposed to serious drawbacks. In behalf of the real or assumed beliefs of the greatest number, the state considers itself bound to impose upon thought terms which thought cannot accept. The belief or the opinion of the one side should not be a fetter upon the other side. As long as the masses were believers, that is to say, as long as the same sentiments were almost universally professed by a people, freedom of research and discussion

[15] Ernest Renan, *Recollections of My Youth,* tr. from the French by C. B. Pitman, and revised by Mme Renan, London: Chapman & Hall, 1883, pp. xiii-xxi.

were impossible. A colossal weight of stupidity pressed down upon the human mind. The terrible catastrophe of the Middle Ages, that break of a thousand years in the history of civilization, is due less to the barbarians than to the triumph of the dogmatic spirit among the masses.

This is a state of things which is coming to an end in our time, and we must not be surprised if some disturbance ensues. There are no longer masses who believe; a great number of the people decline to recognize the supernatural, and the day is not far distant when beliefs of this kind will die out altogether in the masses, just as the belief in familiar spirits and ghosts have disappeared. Even if, as is probable, we are to have a temporary Catholic reaction, the people will not revert to the Church. Religion has become once and for all a matter of personal taste. Now beliefs are only dangerous when they represent something like unanimity or an unquestionable majority. When they are merely individual, there is not a word to be said against them, and it is our duty to treat them with the respect which they do not always exhibit for their adversaries, when they feel that they have force at their back.

There can be no denying that it will take time for the liberty, which is the aim and object of human society, to take root in France as it has in America. French democracy has several essential principles to acquire, before it can become a liberal régime. It will be above all things necessary that we should have laws as to associations, charitable foundations, and the right of legacy, analogous to those which are in force in England and America. Supposing this progress to be effected (if it is utopian to count upon it in France, it is not so for the rest of Europe, in which the aspirations for English liberty become every day more intense), we should really not have much cause to look regretfully upon the favours conferred by the *ancien régime* upon things of the mind.

I quite think that if democratic ideas were to secure a definitive triumph, science and scientfic teaching would soon find the modest subsidies now accorded them cut off. This is an eventuality which would have to be accepted as philosophically as may be. The free foundations would take the place of the state institutes, the slight drawbacks being more than compensated for by the advantage of having no longer to make to the supposed prejudices of the majority concessions which the state exacted in return for its pittance. The waste of power in state institutes is enormous. Private foundations would not be exposed to nearly so much waste. It is true that spurious science would, in these conditions, flourish side by side with real science, enjoying the same privileges, and that there would be no official criterion, as there still is to a certain extent now, to distinguish the one from the other. But this criterion becomes every day less reliable. Reason has to submit to the indignity of taking second place behind those who have a loud voice, and who speak with a tone of command. The plaudits and favour of the public will, for a long time to come, be at the service of what is false. But the true has great power, when it is free; the true endures; the false is ever changing and decays. Thus it is that the true, though only understood by a select few, always rises to the surface, and in the end prevails.

In short, it is very possible that the American-like social condition towards which we are advancing, independently of any particular form of government, will not be more intolerable for persons of intelligence than the better guaranteed social conditions which we have already been subject to. We may at least hope that vulgarity will not yet a while persecute freedom of mind. Descartes, living in the brilliant seventeenth century, was nowhere so well off as at Amsterdam, because, as "everyone was engaged in trade there," no one paid any heed to him. It may be that general vulgarity will one day be the condition of happiness, for the worst American vulgarity would not send Giordano Bruno to the stake or persecute Galileo . . . We shall pass through several alternatives of anarchy and despotism before we find repose in this happy medium. But liberty is like truth; scarcely anyone loves it on its own account, and yet, owing to the impossibility of extremes, one always comes back to it.

— Reading No. 16 —

RENAN: *THE UNITY OF EUROPE*[16]

When the Franco-Prussian war began in the summer of 1870, Renan wrote an article *"La Guerre entre la France et l'Allemagne"* which appeared in the *Revue des Deux Mondes* on September 15, 1870. In this article he foresaw the war's consequences for Europe and Russia—consequences which have since come true.

✓   ✓   ✓

I always regarded the war between France and Germany as the greatest misfortune which could happen to the cause of civilization. . . . In fact, if we leave aside the United States of America whose undoubtedly brilliant future is still obscure and which in any case occupies a secondary rank in the original labor of the human mind, the intellectual and moral greatness of Europe rests on the Triple Alliance of France, Germany and England. Its rupture would be deeply grievous for progress. United, these three great forces would lead the world and lead it well. They would necessarily lead the other elements, each of considerable importance, which compose Europe. They would, above all, imperiously trace a road for another force which one should neither exaggerate nor depreciate—Russia. Russia is a danger only if the rest of Europe abandons her to the false idea of an originality which she perhaps does not possess, and allows her to unite the barbaric peoples of central Asia. These peoples are entirely powerless by themselves, but they are capable of discipline and unity around a Muscovite Genghis Khan if heed is not taken. The United States can become a danger only if a divided Europe allows it to abandon itself to the lures of a presumptuous

[16] Ernest Renan, *La Réforme Intellectuale et Morale*, ed. by P. E. Chavret, Cambridge University Press, 1950, pp. 79-104.

youth and to hold resentments against the motherland.
. . . That was only a dream. One day was sufficient to
overthrow the edifice which housed our hopes and to
open the world to all kinds of dangers, creeds, and
brutalities. . . .

And now who will conclude the peace? . . . The
worst consequence of war is to render powerless those
who did not desire the war. It opens a fatal circle where
common sense is called cowardice and sometimes even
treason. Let us speak frankly. One force alone in the
world will be able to repair the evil which feudal pride,
exaggerated patriotism, the excess of personal power and
the low state of parliamentary government on the continent, has cost to civilization. This force is Europe.
Europe has a major interest that neither of the two
nations should be too victorious or too vanquished. The
disappearance of France from among the great powers
would mean the end of the European balance. I dare
say that Britain especially would feel the conditions of
her existence completely changed when such an event
should happen. France is one of the conditions of Britain's prosperity. The alliance of France and Britain
is well-established for centuries to come. Let Britain
think of the United States, of Constantinople, of India;
she will always find that she needs France and a strong
France. . . .

How could such a horrifying event occur which will
leave a memory of terror connected with the year 1870?
Because the various European nations are too independent from each other and have no authority above
them. There exists neither a congress nor a parliament
which would be superior to national sovereignties.
Though especially since 1814, Europe has acted frankly
as a collective force, the central power has not been
strong enough to prevent terrible wars. It must become
so strong. That dream of pacifist utopians, a code of
justice without an army to uphold its decisions, is a
chimera. Nobody will obey it. On the other hand, the
opinion that peace can be assured when one nation would
have an uncontested superiority over the others is the
opposite of the truth; each nation which exercises hegemony prepares its own ruin by this fact alone, because

it brings about a coalition of all the other countries against itself. Peace cannot be established and maintained except by the common interest of Europe, or, if one prefers it, by a league of neutral powers ready to enforce peace. Justice has no chance to triumph between two contending parties, but between ten contending parties, justice wins out; for she alone offers a common basis of agreement. The only force capable of upholding a decision for the welfare of the European family against its most powerful member state lies in the power of the various states to unite, to intervene and to mediate. Let us hope that this force will assume ever more concrete and regular forms and will lead in the future to a real congress, meeting periodically if not permanently. It will become the heart of the United States of Europe, bound by a federal pact. . .'.

I know there exist in the world foci of fanaticism which are still entirely dominated by temperament. In certain countries a military nobility exists which is fundamentally hostile to reasonableness and which dreams of exterminating whatever does not resemble it. The feudal elements in Prussia and Russia are still at an age in which one possesses the acridity of barbarian blood, an age in which one forbears to look back lest he should fall into disillusionment. France and, to a certain extent, Britain, have achieved their goal. Prussia and Russia have not yet arrived at the satisfaction of their desires, a point at which one can regard coolly the causes for which one has troubled the world. The new and violent races of the North are more naive. They are taken in by their desires. Carried away by the goal which they have proposed to themselves, they resemble a young man who imagines that he will be completely happy once he will have obtained the object of his passion. Add to this the feeling which the sandy plains of northern Germany always seem to have inspired, the feeling of the chaste Vandals confronted by the mores and luxury of the Roman Empire; a kind of Puritan furor, a jealousy and rage against the easy life of those who enjoy life. This somber and fanatical mood still exists today. These melancholic minds believed themselves burdened with the task of avenging virtue and of improving corrupt nations. For these enthusiasts, the idea of the German Reich is not that of a limited nationality, free at home, which does not occupy itself with the rest of the world. What they desire is a universal action of the German race, an action which would renew and dominate Europe.

Their frenzy is chimeric; for let us assume, to please these chagrined minds, that France were destroyed, Belgium, Holland and Switzerland wiped out, and Britain passive and silent: what should we say then of the great ghost which haunts the German future, namely, the Slav race, which would aspire more strongly to separate itself from Germany the more the latter individualizes herself? Slav consciousness grows in proportion to the growth of German consciousness. They oppose each other and create each other. The German has the right to a fatherland like everyone else; but he has no more the right to dominate than anyone else. . . .

The greatest mistake which liberals could make in the midst of the horrors which surround us would be to despair. The future belongs to liberalism. This war, the object of future maledictions, has come because the principles of liberalism have been abandoned, principles which at the same time concern peace and the union of nations. The baneful desire for revenge—a desire which would indefinitely prolong the extermination—will be averted by a wise development of liberal policy. . . .

The immense majority of mankind abhors war. The truly Christian ideas of kindness, justice and goodness conquer the world more and more. The warlike spirit survives only with the professional soldiers and the nobility of northern Germany and Russia. Democracy neither wishes nor understands war. The progress of democracy will bring the end of the reign of these iron men, the survivors of another era, which our century has seen with fear, emerge from the womb of the old Germanic world. . . .

The principle of independent nationalities is not, as some think, capable of freeing mankind from the scourge of war. On the contrary, I have always felt that the principle of nationalities, substituted for the mild and paternal symbol of legitimacy, made the conflicts of nations degenerate into extermination of races, and put an end to those tempers and polite attitudes which the small political and dynastic wars of other times allowed. One will be able to end wars only after joining to the principle of nationalities the one principle which can correct it, the principle of European federation, superior to all the nationalities. Then the democratic questions, differentiated from the questions of pure policy and diplomacy, would regain their importance. . . .

German naturalists who wish to apply their science to politics, maintain, with an unconcern that they wish to regard as profundity, that the law of destruction of races and of the struggle for existence dominates history. They believe that the stronger race necessarily drives out the weaker race, and that the German race, being stronger than the Latin and Slav races, is summoned to defeat and subjugate them. . . . But the animal races which these naturalists have studied do not conclude alliances among themselves. One has never seen two or three races which were in danger of being destroyed form a coalition against their common enemies. The federal principle, the guardian of justice, is the foundation of humanity. It is the guarantee of the rights of all of us. There is no European people which must not bow before such a tribunal. The great German race, greater in reality than its bungling apologists wish to make it appear, will certainly have another high claim for consideration in the future, if one will be able to say that its powerful action has definitely introduced so essential a principle into European law. All the great military hegemonies, that of Spain in the sixteenth century and those of France under Louis XIV and Napoleon, have ended in quick exhaustion. Let Prussia take heed. Her radical policy can engage her in a series of complications from which it will not be easy to disentangle herself. A penetrating eye could perhaps now perceive the formation of future coalitions. The wise friends of Prussia will tell her, not as a threat but as a warning: *vae victoribus,* woe to the victors.

RENAN: *THE PROBLEMS OF PEACE*[17]

After the Franco-Prussian War and the loss of Alsace-Lorraine, Renan wrote a letter, dated September 15, 1871, to his former friend, the German scholar David Friedrich Strauss (1808-1874), who had enthusiastically supported the German war goals.

✓   ✓   ✓

For the last year I have been in the situation of all those who preach moderation in times of crisis. The evidence and the overwhelming majority of public opinion were against me. But I cannot say that I have been converted. Let us wait for ten or fifteen years. I am convinced that the enlightened part of Germany will then recognize that I was its best friend when I advised gentleness in the use of victory. I do not believe that any extreme solutions will last. I would be much surprised if such an absolute faith in the virtue of a race as that professed by Bismarck and Moltke did not end in discomfiture. By abandoning herself to the statesmen and warriors of Prussia, Germany has mounted a frisky horse which will lead her where she does not wish to go. You play for too high stakes. Your conduct exactly resembles that of France at a period with which one reproaches her most. In 1792 the European powers provoked France; France defeated the powers, which was her right; then she pushed her victory to excesses, in which she was wrong. Excess is bad; pride is the only vice which will be punished in this world. To triumph is always a mistake and in any case something which little befits a philosopher. . . .

It is useless to say that sixty or seventy years ago we

---

[17] Ernest Renan, *ibid.,* pp. 119-27.

acted in the same way, and that we then pillaged, mas-
sacred, and conquered in Europe. We have always censured these mistakes of the First Empire. They were the
work of a generation, with which we have little in
common and whose glory is no longer ours. . . . If
one does not admit a statute of limitations for the
violence of the past, there will be endless war. Lorraine
had been part of the German Empire, without doubt;
but Holland, Switzerland, Italy herself, and if we go
back beyond the treaty of Verdun (843), the whole of
France including even Catalonia, formed part of the
German Empire. Alsace today is a German country by
language and race; but before it was invaded by the
Germans, Alsace, like a great portion of southern Germany, was Celtic. We do not conclude from this fact that
southern Germany ought to be French; but we do not
wish to be told that by ancient right Metz and Luxem-
bourg ought to be German. Nobody could say where
this archeology might end. Almost everywhere that the
enthusiastic German patriots claim a German right, we
could claim a previous Celtic right. And before the
Celtic period there were Finnish and Laplandish tribes,
and before them the cave dwellers; and before them
orang-utans. With such a philosophy of history there
would exist no legitimate right in the world except that
of the orang-utans, who were unjustly dispossessed by the
perfidy of the civilized peoples.

Let us be less absolute: besides the right of the dead,
let us admit a little the right of the living. . . . Europe
is a confederation of states united by the common idea
of civilization. The individuality of each nation is constituted without doubt by its race, its language, its history,
its religion, but also by something much more tangible,
by an actual agreement, by the will of the various provinces of a state to live together. Before the unfortunate
annexation of Nice (1860), no part of France wished to
separate herself from France; this was sufficient to make
every dismemberment of France a European crime,
though France was a unity neither in language or race.
On the contrary, parts of Belgium and Switzerland, and
to a general degree the Channel Islands, though they
speak French in no way wish to belong to France. This

is sufficient to make any effort to annex them by force a criminal act. Alsace is German by language and race, but she does not wish to belong to the German state; that settles the question. One speaks of the right of France, of the right of Germany. These abstractions mean much less to us than the right of the Alsatians, living human beings, to obey only a power to which they consent. . . . You have erected in the world a standard of the ethnographical and archeological policy instead of a liberal policy; this policy will be fatal to you. The comparative philology which you have created and which you have wrongly transferred to the political field will bode ill for you.

The Slavs get enthusiastic about it. Every Slav school teacher is becoming your enemy, a termite which ruins your house. How can you believe that the Slavs will not do to you what you are doing to others? The Slav march behind you and follow you step by step. Every affirmation of Germanism is an affirmattion of Slavism. A glance at the affairs of Austria shows that to full evidence. There are twice as many Slavs as Germans. Like the Dragon of the Apocalypse the Slav will one day drag behind him the hordes of Central Asia, the ancient clientele of Genghis Khan and Tamerlane. How much better it would have been for you if you could have reserved for that day the right to appeal to reason, to morality, to friendships based on common principles. Think only how much it will weigh in the balance of the world when one day the Bohemians, the Moravians, the Croatians, the Serbs, all the Slav peoples of the Ottoman Empire, certainly destined for emancipation, young and heroic races filled with military ardor and needing only leadership, will group themselves around the great Muscovite aggregation which already comprises so many diverse elements. . . .

Distrust, therefore, the ethnography; or rather, do not apply it too strongly to the realm of politics. Under the pretext of a German etymology, Prussia annexes the villages of Lorraine. But what will you say if one day the Slavs should come and vindicate Prussia proper: Pomerania, Silesia, Berlin, because their names are Slavic; if they will do on the banks of the Elbe and Oder what you are doing on the banks of the Moselle; when they will point out, on the map, villages which once were inhabited by Slavic tribes? A nation is not synonymous with race. . . . Britain, which is the most nearly perfect of all nations, is the most greatly mixed one from the point of view of ethnography and history. . . . Everyone should beware of what is too excessive or too absolute in his mind. . . . Your German race always has the inclination to believe in Valhalla, but Valhalla will never be the Kingdom of God. With her military splendor, Germany risks losing her true vocation. Let all of us together take up the great and true problems, the social problems, which can be summed up in the following manner: to find a rational organization of mankind which would be as just as is humanly possible.

— Reading No. 18 —

TAINE: FRENCHMEN AND ENGLISHMEN[18]

In the summer of 1871 the University of Oxford conferred honorary degrees upon a German and a French scholar. The Frenchman was Hippolyte Taine, who, as a result of his journey published *Notes on England*. The concluding section of this work compares the French and English national ways of life as they appeared in 1871.

[18] H. Taine, *Notes on England*, tr. by W. F. Rae, Sixth edition, London: Isbister & Co., 1874, pp. 373-77.

One of my friends returned at the same time as my-self, and we compared the result of our observations. Which of the two forms of civilization is the more valuable, that of England or that of France? That is too vague; we must divide and distinguish. Three things are superior in England.

The Political Constitution.—It is stable, and is in no danger, like ours, of being forcibly overturned and re-modelled every twenty years. It is liberal, and permits individuals to take part as actors or assistants in public affairs, instead of regarding them with mere curiosity; it confides their guidance to the upper class, which is best qualified to direct them satisfactorily, and which finds in so doing their natural occupation, in place of withering or being corrupted for want of something to do, as with us. It lends itself without perturbations to continued improvements, and tends in practice to good government, that which pays the most respect to individual initiative, and confides power to the most worthy. The English Three per Cents are at 94; the citizens speak and form associations at pleasure: no Press in the world is equally well informed, nor are any assemblies equally competent.

Religion.—It subordinates rites and dogmas to morality. It inculcates self-government, the supremacy of conscience, the cultivation of the will. It leaves a sufficiently large space to interpretation and to individual sentiment. It is not actually hostile to the spirit of modern science, nor to the tendencies of modern times. Its ministers are married; it founds schools; it approves of action; it does not counsel asceticism. Thus associated with the laity, it has authority over them; a young man entering life, the adult providing for his career, are restrained and guided up to a certain point by a collection of ancient, popular, and fortifying beliefs, which furnish them with rules of conduct and an exalted idea of the world. Among us a young man of twenty, being obliged to frame this rule by and for himself, does not succeed in doing so till late, sometimes does so imperfectly, or never does it at all.

The greatness of the acquired wealth, combined with the increased power of producing and amassing.—Every useful work executed centuries ago, is transmitted and accumulated without loss; England has not been invaded for eight hundred years, and has had no civil war for two centuries. At the present day her capital is several times larger than that of France. The tokens of comfort and opulence are more numerous there than in any other country of the world. Examine the statistics, the calculations of her commerce, of her industry, of her agriculture, of her annual profits. This is true of moral as well as of physical matters; not only does England understand better than France how to manage her public and private affairs, enrich her soil, improve her cattle, superintend a manufacture, clear, colonize, and turn to account distant countries; but she knows still better how to cultivate herself. If we consider but the select few, we shall find, it appears, minds in France of equal calibre, except where politics are concerned, to the most notable minds of England, perhaps even a few superior minds, of wider and of finer mold. But the majority of those with an average intellect, a country gentleman, an ordinary clergyman, is endowed here with more extensive and more solid knowledge. Assuredly, his head is better furnished, his intellectual furniture being less old-fashioned and less incomplete. Above all, the number of persons adequately informed and capable of forming an opinion in political matters is much greater. Compare one of our English clergymen and English gentlemen with the bourgeois and curés of France; or, better still, examine in turn the daily food of their intellects, the English newspaper and the French newspaper, especially a French gazette of a small town and an English gazette of a small town; the distance is prodigious. Now, it is not the select few, it is the average majority which gives the tone, inspires opinion, conducts affairs. On the other hand, three things are better in France.

The Climate.—This is self-evident; yet without personal experience and prolonged reflection it is hard to imagine the effect of six or eight degrees of latitude at the least, in warding off bodily suffering and mental sadness.

The Distribution of Wealth.—There are four or five

millions of landed proprietors in France, and properties after death are divided in equal portions among the children. On the whole, then, our institutions, our habits combine to provide that no one has too large a slice, and that everyone has a small one. Many live poorly, but nearly all can exist without too great difficulty. The wretched are less wretched; the laborer, entirely dependent upon the work of his hands, does not feel that beneath him yawns a dreadful abyss, a black and bottomless pit, in which, owing to an accident, a strike, an attack of sickness, he and his family will be engulfed; having fewer wants and fewer children he bears a lighter burden; besides, want debases him less, and he is less drunken.

Domestic and Social Life.—Several circumstances render it more easy and more enjoyable. In the first place, the natural temperament is gay, more open, and more neighborly. Then the absolute, or nearly absolute, equality established by law or by custom between parents and children, between the eldest son and his younger brothers, between husband and wife, between the noble and the commoner, between the rich and the poor, suppresses much constraint, represses much tyranny, prevents much superciliousness, smooths many asperities. In France, in the narrow domestic circle, the members open their hearts, enter into the spirit of the moment, combine to live together freely and affectionately; in the large social circle, they chat, display a half-confidence, meet together in order to pass an hour freely and pleasantly. There is less constraint at home and in society; kindliness and politeness supplant subordination with advantage. To my mind a human being among us feels less frequently and less heavily the pressure of another rough and despotic human being's hand upon his head. Final cause of expansion: one may say everything in conversation, tell a story and uphold a theory to the end. Romances, criticism, art, philosophy, violent curiosity, have not to submit to the trammels which religion, morality, and official propriety impose upon them across the Channel. At Paris we think with more independence, with a more entire disinterestedness, in a wholly abstract style, without preoccupying ourselves about the consequences, without standing in dread of the thunders of public reprobation.

In fine, all these differences contribute to render the Englishman more powerful and the Frenchman happier. The costume of the former is more substantial; that of the latter more comfortable. The former has reason for enlarging his garment which cramps him at the corners; the latter would act wisely in avoiding those hasty movements which may rend his flimsy material. But it appears to me that each of them has the style of dress which he prefers.

— Reading No. 19 —

MONTALEMBERT: *LIBERAL CATHOLICISM*[19]

After Lacordaire's death, Count de Montalembert published a short biography of the priest who, through his sermons in Notre Dame Cathedral, had attracted many to his attempted reconciliation of the Catholic tradition with modern civilization.

✶   ✶   ✶

Lacordaire belongs to that race of rare and strong-minded men, who, born on the confines of two centuries, have, despite faults and weaknesses, redeemed

[19] Count de Montalembert, *Memoir of the Abbé Lacordaire,* authorized translation, London: Richard Bentley, 1863, pp. 3, 4, 6, 102-05, 129-30, 209, 219, 239, 259, 260-62, 263, 265-69.

France from her crimes, and raised her from the dust: who have honoured and elevated the French mind, who have inaugurated, instead of the triumphs of the spirit of usurpation and conquest, a period of enlightenment, of liberty, of public and intellectual life, of Catholic regeneration. The name of Lacordaire will pale before none of the great names which have presided at this great political and religious resurrection.

Born at the beginning of this century, he knew all its trials and all its greatness. Born a democrat, and nursed in republican ideas, he early circumscribed, without ever extinguishing it, that revolutionary lava which from time to time burst forth in his discourses, no longer to spread ruin and dismay, but to serve as a beacon in the surrounding night.

When he became a believer, a Catholic, a priest, and a monk, he betrayed no single one of the rightful instincts and generous convictions of his youth. . . .

And yet, sad and strange to say, he, the greatest of priests, and the purest of democrats, was never adopted by democracy, nor ever thoroughly understood and appreciated by the clergy. . . .

Lacordaire was asked to give conferences to the scholars of the most unpretending of the Paris colleges, the Collège Stanislas. They were begun on the 19th of January, 1834: at the second, the chapel was unable to hold the crowd that pressed in, and a gallery had to be erected. . . .

But still he met with marked and continually increasing opposition. "Here," he wrote, towards the close of this first series of conferences, "I am looked upon as a hare-brained republican, an incorrigible offender, and a thousand other delicate things of the same sort. . . . There are some ecclesiastics who charge me, not precisely with atheism, but with not having pronounced the name of Jesus Christ one single time. . . . I scorn the annoyance given to me: I fulfill my duty as a man and a priest: I live alone, in continual study, calm, trustful in God and the future. Nothing can be done without the help of the Church and of time. Had the Abbé de Lamennais but willed, what a glorious opening for him! He was at the height of his glory, and I have never been able to understand how a man of that cast could have ignored the value of what God left for him. The religious task forsaken by him is so grand, so easy, so much above all others, that in three months, in Paris, I have moved more hearts and heads than I could possibly have done during the fifteen years of the Restoration."

Upon the repeated instances of a deputation of law students, the Archbishop called upon the preacher of the Collège Stanislas to mount the pulpit of Notre-Dame, and to give the conferences which had been organized for the youth of the schools the preceding year without any great result.

Lacordaire ascended, then, for the first time that pulpit since immortalized by him, and delivered during the years 1835 and 1836 the fifteen famous conferences which are in everybody's hands. . . .

"We both served Christian freedom under the standard of public freedom," said Lacordaire, with happy terseness in his notice upon Father de Ravignan. The latter, in an eloquent, calm, and dignified publication, demanded as a citizen, and in the name of that liberty of conscience guaranteed to all, the right to be and to call himself a Jesuit. Lastly, the illustrious priest who has since won the first place among the episcopacy of our day, spoke as follows, with the universal assent of the clergy and faithful:

"What is meant by the spirit of the French Revolution? . . . Are we to understand free institutions, liberty of conscience, political liberty, civil and individual liberty, the liberty of families, freedom of education, liberty of opinion, equality before the law, the equal distribution of public taxes and burdens?

"All this, we not only honestly accept, but all this we call for in the broad daylight of public discussion. These liberties, so dear to those who charge us with not loving them, we champion; we ask them for ourselves as well as for others. At the present moment what are we doing, other than rendering homage to the true spirit of the French Revolution, by claiming its advantages, and demanding the freedom of instruction promised by the Charta, in the name of every lawful religious liberty? . . ."

Born a democrat, Lacordaire had no difficulty in believing, like all the clear-headed men of this age, in the inevitable triumph of democracy; but he espoused neither its extreme tendencies, nor its bad quarrels. Like the majority of real liberals, he was tolerably indifferent to dynastic questions, and in a certain measure, to forms of government. He always, however, leant towards limited monarchy. . . .

Between a constitutional monarchy and a republic the difference is superficial; whilst between a constitutional and an absolute monarchy the difference is fundamental. Consequently Lacordaire could, without inconsistency, hail the advent of the Republic with confidence and joy. He associated himself with that group of fervent Catholics who believed that 1848 was the dawn of a New Era. They gave their paper this name, preached in it the acceptance of the new state of things, and proclaimed the necessary connection between Christianity and democracy with an honest but intemperate zeal which was not shared in, but could not sufficiently be got under by him who had so eloquently combatted the doctrine of the necessary connection between Catholicism and monarchy. . . .

Lacordaire was ever hoping to see the pontiff enter spontaneously, and of his own authority, into the way of reforms, and thus form in Italy an honest and enlightened Christian party. "I am for the Holy See against its oppressors; I believe in the moral necessity of its temporal power, I compassionate with its misfortunes, I would willingly give the last drop of my blood for it; but, at the same time, I desire the freedom of Italy, serious changes in the government of the Papal States, and a still more important change in that moral direction which, in these later times, the *Univers* and the *Civiltà Cattolica* represent. . . ."

His last discourse (1854) contained, upon the moral misery of nations, fallen from the high estate of political freedom, and reduced to what he called private life, certain outbursts of truth, grief, and offended honesty, which were out of season. He had finally to give up preaching in public. . . . I do not believe that any formal prohibition, even from the temporal power, was ever signified

to him; but there was a kind of general feeling that that
bold and free voice, which had been heard for twenty
years, under all kinds of governments, without ever being checked, and with no other curb than that of orthodoxy, was no longer in place. . . . The great orator had
to complain of no violence, no persecution; and I do
but state the truth in saying that I never detected in
him the slightest tinge of bitterness or animosity towards
the new government. That government prompted him
simply to a dignified neutrality, if anything, slightly dis-
tainful, as was his wont with regard to all governments.

But the country! public opinion, the multitude! That
country which he supposed to be panting after every
liberty! That opinion which he had seen so excited, so
ready, not only for resistance, but for revolt! Those mul-
titudes but lately so rebellious to all authority, even the
mildest, suddenly become eager not only to accept but
to cry out for a master. Alas! what a bitter disenchant-
ment for his patriotism! . . .

But what was this purely political wound in comparison with that which pierced his priestly heart, at the
sight of the attitude taken up by Catholics, and a too
large portion of the clergy! How should he have been
otherwise than astounded and broken-hearted? He saw
that clergy suddenly fall a prey to an unpardonable illusion, and to a prostration unexampled in the history of
the Church. Names which had the honour to figure beside his own in those memorable manifestoes in which
Christian freedom was invoked under the shadow of
public liberty, suddenly appeared at the foot of orations
and pastorals, which borrowed the forms of Byzantine
adulation in order to greet the mad dream of an orthodox absolutism.

All the cynicism of political apostasy was acted over
again and outdone by the shameful ranting of the principal organs of Catholic opinion in the press: "The
Ultramontane school," wrote the Archbishop of Paris,
"was lately a school of liberty; it has been turned into a
school of slavery, which is attempting to bring about a
double idolatry, the idolatry of the temporal and the
idolatry of the spiritual power."

Those who had so loudly claimed common rights and

liberty for all, who had so boldly declared that liberty was both the cry of the Church in its infancy, and the cry of victorious humanity, and that the people of February 1848 had the divine sentiment of the natural alliance between Catholicism and liberty; these very men pretended to concur in or at least to assist at the restoration of what they called Christian monarchy, and, under this pretence, they were to be seen exculpating at the same time the Roman empire and the first French empire, crying down all the rights of political liberty, loudly calling in force to the assistance of the faith, affirming that the yoke of the law of God must be forced upon all; lauding and regretting the Inquisition; declaring the ideal principle of liberty to be anti-Christian; even civil tolerance to be crime; finally, shamelessly putting forth that in claiming under Louis Philippe general liberty, they had simply meant their own, and, "that liberty of conscience ought to be restricted in proportion as truth prevailed." . . .

One may easily imagine the horror with which such speedy and such black ingratitude towards freedom was calculated to strike him, who, from the pulpit of Notre-Dame, had, in presence of his archbishop, and without a single Catholic voice being raised to gainsay or warn him, thus enunciated the language of justice and honor: —"Whoever in his cry for right, excepts a single man; whoever consents to the slavery of a single man, be he white or black, were it only to extend to the unlawful binding of a single hair of his head; that man is not sincere, and deserves not to fight for the sacred cause of the human race. Public conscience will always repel the man who asks for exclusive liberty, or forgets the rights of others; for exclusive liberty is but a privilege, and a liberty forgetful of others' rights is nothing better than treason . . . But there is in the heart of the honest man who speaks for all, and who, in speaking for all, sometimes seems to be speaking against himself, there is in that man a power, a logical and moral superiority, which almost infallibly begets reciprocity. Yes, Catholics, know this well: if you want liberty for yourselves, you must will it for all men under heaven. If you ask it for yourselves simply, it will never be granted; give it where you are masters, in order that it may be given you there where you are slaves."

— Reading No. 20 —

VEUILLOT: *ULTRAMONTANE CATHOLICISM*[20]

In 1866 Louis Veuillot published a pamphlet in which he advanced his opposition to liberal Catholicism. Veuillot maintained that the liberal illusion is not only empty, but that its counsels to the Catholic world of a reconciliation with modern civilization are weak and dishonest recommendations which disclose the ignoble mainspring of liberal Catholicism.

✓   ✓   ✓

The children of the Christ, the children of the King, are kings. They form an absolutely superior society, whose duty it is to take possession of the earth and reign over it for the purpose of baptizing all men and of raising them to that selfsame supernatural life, that selfsame royalty and that selfsame glory for which Christ has destined them. They ought to strive for that goal, because the only way of realizing the ideal of universal liberty, universal equality, universal fraternity is to establish the universal reign of Christ. For the liberty that is man's due is liberty to attain his supernatural end, which

[20] Louis Veuillot, *The Liberal Illusion,* tr. by George Barry O'Toole, Washington, 1939. Reprinted by permission of the publisher, pp. 37-38, 38-39, 47-48, 62-64, 76-77.

is union with Christ; and the only society ever known to recognize all men as equals and as brothers is the society of the disciples of Christ.

In the normal order, Christian society is maintained and extended by means of two powers that ought to be distinct—not separated, united—not confused, one above the other—not equal. The one is the head, the other the arm; the one is the supreme and sovereign word of the Pontiff, the other the social power. . . .

These two powers, united, distinct and one above the other, whereby Christian society is ruled, have been called the two swords. For the word would be of no avail, if it could not be at certain moments a sword. The meekness of Christ has willed that there should be two swords, so that the advent of repression might be delayed and the need of it forestalled.

The first sword, the one that cleaves nothing but darkness, remains in the patient and infallibly enlightened power of the Pontiff. The other, the material sword, is in the hand of the representative of society, and in order that it may make no mistake, it is in duty bound to obey the commandment of the Pontiff. It is the Pontiff who bids it come forth from the scabbard and who bids it return thereto. Its duty is to repress aggressive error, once it has been defined and condemned, to shackle it, to strike it down; to give protection to the truth, whether the latter is under the necessity of defending itself, or has need in its turn, to go on the offensive. . . .

The Christians despoiled pagan society of its weapons and its temples to transform them, not to destroy them. From the temple, they expelled the idol; upon might they imposed right. The foolish idea of abolishing force never even came to them. Force allowed itself to be transposed, allowed itself to be disciplined; allowed itself to be sanctified. Who is so rash as to think he can abolish might? and why, after all, should anyone wish to abolish it at all? Might is a very good thing; it is a gift of God, nay a very attribute of God, "I am the most mighty God of thy father."

As right is of itself a force, so force can be of itself a right. Mankind and the Church recognize a right of war. From the iron of which it despoiled barbarous force,

Christianity made coats of mail for the weak and noble swords with which it armed the right. Force in the hands of the Church is the force of right, and we have no desire that right should remain without force. Force in its proper place and doing its duty, that is the orderly way.

Because in the present world force is not everywhere in its proper place, that is to say at the disposition of the Church; because often, far from serving right, it is abused against the right, shall we therefore say yes to the illuminati, some of whom decree the outright abolition of force, while the rest ordain that the supreme right shall never have force at its disposal, for fear it might hamper the liberty that wants to destroy the truth?

We ought, on the contrary, to be ready to shed our blood in order to restore force to its lawful function, in order to attach it exclusively to the service of right.

Force ought to protect, to affirm, to vindicate the grandest, the noblest, the most necessary right of man, which is to acknowledge and to serve God; it should enable the Church to extend to every man on earth the benefit of this right. Let us never relinquish this right which liberal Catholicism surrenders, so that it can drift down the current, along with the crowd. . . .

The revolutionary sphinx, under the name of the modern mind, propounds a series of riddles with which the liberal Catholics occupy themselves a great deal more than befits the dignity of children of Christ. Not one of them, however, answers the riddle in a way calculated to satisfy either the sphinx, or themselves, or anybody else, and it is a matter of record, that the monster devours soonest just those who flatter themselves on having guessed its meaning best.

Scant is the self-respect and scant the faith that remains in these last! They come, not without arrogance, to ask, in the name of the sphinx and in their own name, how "intolerant" Catholics can get around the "conquests" of the dissenting mind with its rights of man, its liberty of religions, its constitutions grounded on these principles, etc., etc. Nothing could be easier to answer.

To begin with, the dissenting mind invariably starts off

with an unwarranted assumption of its own superiority, which we flatly refuse to recognize. Error is never the equal, much less the superior of truth, neither can it hope to overawe truth, or ever to prevail legitimately against it, and, by consequence, the disciples of error, infidels, unbelievers, atheists, renegades and the like, are never the superiors nor even the legitimate equals of the disciples of Jesus Christ, the one true God. From the standpoint of unalterable right, the perfect society that constitutes the Church of Christ is by no means on a level with the gang that collects around error. We know right well to whom it has been said: Going thereforth, teach—a word, we may remark in passing, like the great Increase and multiply, which was spoken at the beginning of things; and these two words are living words despite the ruses and triumphs of death—error has nothing to teach by divine right, neither has it the divine right to increase and multiply. Truth is at liberty to tolerate error, but error is obliged to grant to truth the right of liberty. . . .

In a word, Catholic society will be Catholic, and the dissenters whom it will tolerate will know its charity, but they will not be allowed to disrupt its unity.

This is the answer that Catholics can, on their part, make to the sphinx; and these are the words that will kill it outright. The sphinx is not invulnerable; against it we have just what is required in the way of weapons. The Archangel did not overcome the Rebel with material weapons, but with this word: Who is like unto God! And Satan fell, struck as by a bolt of lightning. . . .

It is only too evident that, considering the present state of the world, liberal Catholicism has no value whatever either as a doctrine or as a means of defending religion; that it is powerless to insure for the Church a peace which would bring her the least advancement or glory. It is nothing but an illusion, nothing but a piece of stubbornness—a pose. One can predict its fate. Abandoned in the near future by generous minds, to whom it may provide a certain outlet for sentiment, it will go on to merge itself with the general body of heresy. The adherents whom it drags after it may then be turned into fanatical persecutors, in keeping with the usual in-

consistency of weak intellects obsessed with the false
spirit of conciliation! Certain minds seem to be as sus-
ceptible to error as certain constitutions to disease.
Everything that is unwholesome finds lodgment in them;
they are carried away by the very first wind and en-
snared by the very first sophism; they are the property,
the booty, the chattels of the powers of darkness, and
one may define them as antiquity defined slaves, *non
tam biles quam nulli*—"not so much vile beings as no-
bodies."

Let us undertake not so much to convince them as to
set them an example that may save them.

In harmony with faith, reason exhorts us to unite and
make ourselves strong in obedience. To whom shall we
go? Liberals or not liberals, beset with the terrible per-
plexities of these troublous times, we know only one
thing for a certainty: it is that no man knows anything,
except the man with whom God is for aye, the man who
possesses the thought of God.

It behooves us to lock arms around the Sovereign
Pontiff, to follow unswervingly his inspired directions,
to affirm with him the truths that alone can save our
souls and the world. It behooves us to abstain from any
attempt to twist his words to our own sense: "When
the Sovereign Pontiff has proclaimed a pastoral decision,
no one has the right to add or to suppress the smallest
vowel, no addere, no minuere. Whatever he affirms, that
is true forever." Any other course can but result in dividing us further and in fatally disrupting our unity. That
is the misfortune of misfortunes. The doctrines known
as liberal have riven us apart. Before their inroad, favored only too much, alas! by a spell of political bad
humor, few as we were, we amounted, nevertheless, to
something: we formed an unbroken phalanx. We rallied
in such a phalanx whenever we chose to do so; it was
no more than a pebble if you will: that pebble had at
least its compactness and its weight. Liberalism has shat-
tered it and reduced it to so much dust. I doubt if it
still holds its place: dispersal is not expansion. At all
events, a hundred thousand pecks of dust would not
furnish ammunition for a single sling. Let us aim now
at but one goal, let us work with but one mind to attain

ıt: let us throw ourselves wholeheartedly into obedience; it will give us the cohesion of rock, and upon this rock, *hanc petram,* Truth shall plant her victorious foot.

— Reading No. 21 —

SOREL: *HEROIC SOCIALISM*²¹

Georges Sorel rejected the piecemeal methods of gradual reform. He believed in the imposition of a new moral order on a disintegrating society through a new ethics of violence. This ethic, to be put into effect by the producers, deeply influenced twentieth-century totalitarianism.

✔   ✔   ✔

The principal reason which prevented the Socialists from studying ethical problems as they deserved was the democratic superstition which has dominated them for so long and which has led them to believe that above everything else the aim of their actions must be the acquisition of seats in political assemblies.

From the moment one has anything to do with elections, it is necessary to submit to certain general conditions which impose themselves unavoidably on all parties in every country and at all times. If one is convinced that the future of the world depends on the electoral programme, on compromises between influential men and

²¹ Georges Sorel, *Reflections on Violence,* tr. by T. E. Hulme and J. Roth, with an introduction by Edward A. Shils, Glencoe, Illinois: the Free Press, 1950, pp. 247-51, 254-58, 264, 267-69, 276-78. Reprinted by permission.

on the sale of privileges, it is not possible to pay much attention to the moral constraints which prevent a man going in the direction of his most obvious interests. Experience shows that in all countries where democracy can develop its nature freely, the most scandalous corruption is displayed without anyone thinking it even necessary to conceal his rascality. Tammany Hall of New York has always been cited as the most perfect type of democratic life, and in the majority of our large towns politicians are found who ask for nothing better than to follow the paths of confreres in America . . .

There is a great resemblance between the electoral democracy and the Stock Exchange; in one case as in the other it is necessary to work upon the simplicity of the masses, to buy the co-operation of the most important papers, and to assist chance by an infinity of trickery. There is not a great deal of difference between a financier who puts big sounding concerns on the market which come to grief in a few years, and the politician who promises an infinity of reforms to the citizens which he does not know how to bring about, and which resolve themselves simply into an accumulation of Parliamentary papers. Neither one nor the other knows anything about production, and yet they manage to obtain control over it, to misdirect and exploit it shamelessly; they are dazzled by the marvels of modern industry, and it is their private opinion that the world is so rich that they can rob it on a large scale without causing any great outcry among the producers; the great art of the financier and the politician is to be able to bleed the taxpayer without bringing him to the point of revolt. . . .

The "new school" is rapidly differentiating itself from official Socialism in recognising the necessity of the improvement of morals . . . In its insatiable desire for reality, it tries to arrive at the real roots of this process of moral perfection and desires to know how to create today the ethic of the producers of the future.

At the beginning of my research on modern ethics this question must be asked: Under what conditions is regeneration possible? The Marxists are absolutely right in laughing at the Utopists and in maintaining that morality is never created by mild preaching, by the ingenious constructions of theorists, or by fine gestures. Proudhon, having neglected this problem, suffered from many illusions about the persistence of the forces which gave life to his own ethics; experience was soon to prove that his undertaking was to remain fruitless. And if the contemporary world does not contain the roots of a new ethic, what will happen to it? The sighs of a whimpering middle class will not save it, if it has forever lost its morality.

Very shortly before his death Renan was much engrossed with the ethical future of the world: "Moral values decline, that is a certainty, sacrifice has almost disappeared; one can see the day coming when everything will be syndicalized, when organized selfishness will take the place of love and devotion. There will be strange upheavals. The two things which alone until now have resisted the decay of reverence, the army and the church, will soon be swept away in the universal torrent." Renan showed a remarkable insight in writing this at the very moment when so many futile intellects were announcing the renascence of idealism and foreseeing progressive tendencies in a church that was at length reconciled with the modern world. But all his life Renan had been too favoured by fortune not to be optimistic; he believed, therefore, that the evil of the future would consist simply in the necessity of passing through a bad period, and he added: "No matter, the resources of humanity are infinite. The eternal designs will be fulfilled, the springs of life ever forcing their way to the surface will never be dried up." . . . If, as Renan asserts, history rewards the resigned abnegation of men who strive uncomplainingly, and who accomplish, without profit, a great historical work, we have a new reason for believing it in the advent of Socialism, since it represents the highest moral ideal ever conceived by man. This time it is not a new religion which is shaping itself underground, without the help of the middle-class thinkers, it is the birth of a virtue, a virtue which the middle-class intellectuals are incapable of understanding, a virtue which has the power to save civilization, as Renan hoped it would be saved—but by the total elimination of the class to which Renan belonged.

. . . Renan himself had lived all his life under the

influence of the sentiment of sublimity inculcated in him by his mother; we know, in fact, that Madame Renan was a woman of lofty character. But the source of sublimity is dried up: "Religious people live on a shadow. We live on the shadow of a shadow. On what will those who come after us live?"

Renan, as was his wont, tried to mitigate the gloom of the outlook which his perspicacity presented to him; he is like many other French writers who, wishing to please a frivolous public, never dare to go to the bottom of the problems that life presents; he does not wish to frighten his amiable lady admirers, so he adds, therefore, that it is not necessary to have a religion burdened with dogmas, such a religion, for example, as Christianity; the religious sentiment should suffice. . . .

"On what will those who come after us live?" This is the great problem posed by Renan and which the middle classes will never be able to solve. If any doubt is possible on this point, the stupidities uttered by the official moralists would show that the decadence is henceforth fatal. Speculations on the harmony of the Universe (even when the Universe is personified) are not the kind of thing which will give men that courage which Renan compared to that of the soldier in the moment of attack. Sublimity is dead in the middle classes, and they are doomed to possess no ethic in the future. . . .

We know with what force Nietzsche praised the values constructed by the masters, by a superior class of warriors who, in their expeditions, enjoying to the full freedom from all social constraint, return to the simplicity of mind of a wild beast, become once more triumphant monsters who continually bring to mind "the superb blond beast, prowling in search of prey and bloodshed," in whom "a basis of hidden bestiality needs from time to time a purgative." To understand this thesis properly, we must not attach too much importance to formulas which have at times been intentionally exaggerated, but should examine the historical facts; the author tells us that he has in mind "the aristocracy of Rome, Arabia, Germany, and Japan, the Homeric heroes, the Scandinavian Vikings." . . .

I believe that if the professor of philology had not

been continually cropping up in Nietzsche he would have perceived that the master type still exists under our own eyes, and that it is this type which, at the present time, has created the extraordinary greatness of the United States. He would have been struck by the analogies which exist between the Yankee, ready for any kind of enterprise, and the ancient Greek sailor, sometimes a pirate, sometimes a colonist or merchant; above all, he would have established a parallel between the ancient heroes and the man who sets out on the conquest of the Far West. . . .

The problem that we shall now try to solve is the most difficult of all those which a Socialist writer can touch upon. We are about to ask how it is possible to conceive the transformation of the men of to-day into the free producers of to-morrow working in manufactories where there are no masters. . . .

Renan asked what was it that moved the heroes of great wars. "The soldier of Napoleon was well aware that he would always be a poor man, but he felt that the epic in which he was taking part would be eternal, that he would live in the glory of France." The Greeks had fought for glory; the Russians and the Turks seek death because they expect a chimerical paradise. "A soldier is not made by promises of temporal rewards. He must have immortality. In default of paradise, there is glory, which is itself a kind of immortality."

Economic progress goes far beyond the individual life, and profits future generations more than those who create it; but does it give glory? Is there an economic epic capable of stimulating the enthusiasm of the workers? The inspiration of immortality which Renan considered so powerful is obviously without efficacy here, because artists have never produced masterpieces under the influence of the idea that their work would procure them a place in paradise (as Turks seek death that they may enjoy the happiness promised by Mahomet). The workmen are not entirely wrong when they look on religion as a middle-class luxury, since, as a matter of fact, the emotions it calls up are not those which inspire workmen with the desire to perfect machinery, or which create methods of accelerating labor.

The question must be stated otherwise than Renan put it; do there exist among the workmen forces capable of producing enthusiasm equivalent to those of which Renan speaks, forces which could combine with the ethics of good work, so that in our days, which seem to many people to presage the darkest future, this ethic may acquire all the authority necessary to lead society along the path of economic progress? . . .

. . . There is only one force which can produce today that enthusiasm without whose coöperation no morality is possible, and that is the force resulting from the propaganda in favour of a general strike. The preceding explanations have shown that the idea of the general strike (constantly rejuvenated by the feelings roused by proletarian violence) produces an entirely epic state of mind, and at the same time bends all the energies of the mind to that condition necessary to the realization of a workshop carried on by free men, eagerly seeking the betterment of the industry; we have thus recognized that there are great resemblances between the sentiments arousd by the idea of the general strike and those which are necessary to bring about a continued progress in methods of production. We have then the right to maintain that the modern world possesses that prime mover which is necessary to the creation of the ethics of the producers.

I stop here, because it seems to me that I have accomplished the task which I imposed upon myself; I have, in fact, established that proletarian violence has an entirely different significance from that attributed to it by superficial scholars and by politicians. In the total ruin of institutions and of morals there remains something which is powerful, new, and intact, and it is that which constitutes, properly speaking, the soul of the revolutionary proletariat. Nor will this be swept away in the general decadence of moral values, if the workers have enough energy to bar the road to the middle-class corrupters, answering their advances with the plainest brutality. . . .

The bond which I pointed out in the beginning of this inquiry between Socialism and proletarian violence appears to us now in all its strength. It is to violence that Socialism owes those high ethical values by means of which it brings salvation to the modern world.

— Reading No. 22 —

JAURÈS: *INTERNATIONAL PEACE* [22]

On November 5, 1911, Germany and France reached an agreement which peacefully closed the second Morocco crisis. The French Chamber of Deputies debated ratification of the treaty on December 20, 1911, and Jean Jaurès delivered a speech there on the bases of international peace. Uttered on the eve of World War I, many of the thoughts of the leader of French socialism apply equally well to the situation today.

Gentlemen, we should not only carry out wise policies in favor of the indigenous of Morocco, but also in favor of all countries and all citizens with whom we keep up relations. On the day after the treaty is signed, all of the contracting parties naturally feel tempted, when explaining the clauses of the treaty to their citizens, to exaggerate the advantages they have gained and to play down any concessions they had to make. . . . If we want the agreement to last we cannot use pressure tactics but must keep it with integrity and in a spirit of complete loyalty.

But no matter what we do, gentlemen, we remain sur-

[22] *Oeuvres de Jean Jaurès, Pour la Paix, Europe Incertaine,* Paris: Rieder, 1934, pp. 423-434—also Jaurès, *Pages Choisies,* Paris: Rieder, 1922, pp. 434-42.

rounded by an atmosphere of suspicion and defiance from which, it seems to me, the clouds of war may descend upon us at any minute. As far as it is our responsibility, as far as it is the responsibility of a great people, we must constantly apply ourselves to dissipate this atmosphere of defiance and to combat the causes of the renewed danger of conflicts. It is our primary duty to reject the pessimism and the fatalism of those who say that war is inevitable.

Gentlemen, I do not disregard the forces for war in this world; but one also has to see and to recognize the forces for peace and to salute them. In its own way, war fosters peace—since the horrors of a modern war are frightening. Gentlemen, when one sometimes speaks lightly of the possibility of this terrible catastrophe one forgets the hitherto unknown extent of the horror and greatness of the disaster that would occur. . . .

The present-day armies of each nation represent entire peoples, as in the times of primitive barbarism; but this time they would be let loose amidst all the complexity and wealth of human civilization. Each of these nations would employ the instruments of terrifying destruction created by modern science. Do not imagine that it will be a short war, consisting of a few thunderbolts and flashes of lightning. On the contrary, there will be slow and formidable collisions like the ones which have taken place over there in Manchuria between the Russians and the Japanese. Untold numbers of human beings will suffer from the sickness, the distress, the pain, the ravages of this multiple explosion. The sick will die of fever; commerce will be paralyzed; factories will stop working; oceans, which steamboats nowadays cross in every direction, will again be empty and silent as in former times.

This terrible spectacle will over-stimulate all human passions. Listen to the words of a man who is passionately attached to the ideals of his party and who is convinced that we must revolutionize our form of property holding, but who also believes that it will be the greatness of this movement to proceed in an evolutionary manner, without unleashing the destructive hatreds which have hitherto accompanied all great movements for social reform throughout history. But we must watch out, for it is in the fever of wars that passions for social reform are aroused to a paroxysm of violence. It was during the War of 1870 and the siege of Paris that convulsions seized that city; it was during the Russo-Japanese War that the fever broke out in Russia. Therefore, the conservatives should be the ones who desire peace more than any others, for once peace is broken the forces of chaos will be let loose. . . .

There are three active forces which I consider to be working for peace today. The first of these is the international organization of the working class of all countries. . . . Nowadays there is yet another force in the world which is working for peace, namely, modern capitalism. . . . Little by little types of property holdings are being transformed. Industrial property has superseded landed property; individually owned industrial property has been changed to the ownership of stocks and bonds. Property moves with the speed and freedom of the migrating birds. Capital passes from the hand of one business to the hand of another, and the corporations grow and expand.

Business interests interact more and more and are becoming more diversified, more fluid and more entangled with each other. Industrial and financial capitalism coöperates across national frontiers. Moreover, the banks operate behind the scenes as sleeping partners of the businesses which they subsidize. As partners and as subsidizers they coördinate these enterprises, while at the same time, they subsidize distant branches in foreign countries and across the seas. Here we see the growing power of the banks, which coördinate investments and entangle interests in such a way that when a single link is broken in Paris credit totters in Hamburg and New York. This is the beginning of capitalist solidarity, which can be dangerous if it is not . . . controlled by public opinion or by independent governments. If, however, it is controlled, enlightened, and watched over by great, independent and proud nations, it might help bring peace to the world in times of instability.

There is, however, a third force for peace in the world: it is Anglo-Saxon America, reborn from the old

Puritan ideals. Gentlemen, we do not know the great American people or the American conscience. We only see their dollar-mindedness; we only see men obsessed by millions, by business, and by gold. There are signs which indicate that the Americans have overcome their crisis; these signs indicate that the millionaires, at the peak of their magnificent fortunes, have experienced the emptiness of horizons which reflect nothing but gold, and now seek nobler food for their thought and spirit. . . . Therefore we find in America a revival of idealism which is not only a surface manifestation, since it digs beneath the dollar era and the period of mercantile materialism to find America's Puritan soul which has its roots in the enthusiasm of the Biblical prophets, and which, in its manner, has dreamed of a free and just society.

It is under the inspiration of these memories, it is by the light of this reborn idealism, that President Taft accomplished those acts which we only half understand because we isolate them from this vast and profound movement. That explains the system of arbitration treaties between the United States and England and between the United States and Japan, which is now beginning to take shape. Oh! this has not been done without resistance, but this resistance proves that these acts are not a dream or a polite expression, but a political, moral and social reality which, like all superior realities, must exert itself and fight in order to establish itself. The most powerful modern orator, Daniel Webster, spoke on behalf of the United States when he cried out against the endeavors and despotism of the Holy Alliance, warning Europe in 1820: "You who have taught us the meaning of liberty, do not fall into servitude!" Should Europe be foolish enough to divide and tear itself apart tomorrow, this great enlightened American idealism would shame it with its proposals for arbitration. . . .

We are told: "So you want to isolate yourselves; you want to remain neutral between England and Germany?" We are warned against neutralism: "Even England had to give up its splendid isolation, for this only brought about dangers." No, gentlemen, there is no question of lessening our ties with England. There are many Englishmen who, just as we do, passionately want the Anglo-French entente to be definitely oriented toward peaceful ends. Sir Edward Grey himself, emphasizing his devotion to a friendship with France, said that now that the Moroccan question has been settled, he hopes that the Anglo-French entente would continue to exist in order to foster the general and permanent aims of justice, civilization and peace. He also added: we are only allied with our friends in just causes, and neither of the two people can be held to follow the other in aggressive ideas or adventures.

Well, gentlemen, England is an immense nation of producers, democrats, workers, and peasants, who all feel the greatness of today's social achievements and who understand that tomorrow's accomplishments depend on a state of peace. We can best serve the Anglo-French entente and those who are enlightened enough to take its aims to heart, by pursuing a mild and conciliatory policy towards Germany, a sign of our love of peace. This is the aim for which we want to clear the ground of all immediate difficulties, to build a temporary edifice of peace and justice. That is why I will vote for the Franco-German agreement. Yet it can be of value only as a prelude, as a protest against the supposed inevitability of war.

A SHORT BIBLIOGRAPHY

Artz, Frederick B., *France Under the Bourbon Restoration, 1814-1830,* Cambridge: Harvard University Press, 1931.

Barzun, Jacques, *The French Race,* New York: Columbia University Press, 1932.

Brinton, Crane, *A Decade of Revolution, 1789-1799,* New York: Harper & Co., 1934.

———— *The Jacobins, An Essay in the New History,* New York: Macmillan, 1930.

Brogan, Denis, *France Under the Republic: the Development of Modern France (1870-1938),* New York and London: Harper & Co., 1940.

———— *French Personalities and Problems,* London: H. Hamilton, 1946.

Bruun, Geoffrey, *Europe and the French Imperium, 1799-1814,* New York: Harper & Co., 1938.

Dansette, Adrian, "Catholicism in France," in *The Catholic Church in World Affairs,* ed. by W. Gurian and M. A. Fitzsimons, Notre Dame: Notre Dame University Press, 1954.

Earle, Edward Mead, *Modern France,* Princeton: Princeton University Press, 1951.

Evans, David Owen, *Social Romanticism in France, 1830-1848,* Oxford: Clarendon Press, 1951.

Faguet, Emile, *Politicians and Moralists of the Nineteenth Century,* Boston: Little, Brown & Co., 1928.

Fisher, H. A. L., *Bonapartism; Six lectures delivered in the University of London,* Oxford: Clarendon Press, 1908.

Guérard, Albert, *French Civilization in the Nineteenth Century; a Historical Introduction,* New York: Century Co., 1914.

Guérard, Albert, *French Prophets of Yesterday; a Study of Religious Thought Under the Second Empire,* London: T. F. Unwin, 1913.

———— *Reflections on the Napoleonic Legend,* New York: Scribner's Sons, 1924.

Hackett, C. A., *Anthology of Modern French Poetry, from Baudelaire to the Present Day,* New York: Macmillan, 1952.

Hales, E. E. Y., *Pio Nono. A Study in European Politics and Religion in the Nineteenth Century,* New York: P. J. Kenedy & Sons, 1954.

Kohn, Hans, *Prophets and Peoples,* New York: Macmillan, 1946.

Laski, Harold, *Authority in the Modern State,* New Haven: Yale University Press, 1919.

McKay, Donald, ed. and translator, *The Dreyfus Case,* New Haven: Yale University Press, 1937.

———— *The United States and France,* Cambridge: Harvard University Press, 1951.

Muret, Mrs. Charlotte, *French Royalist Doctrines Since the Revolution,* New York: Columbia University Press, 1933.

Palmer, R. R., *Twelve Who Ruled; the Committee of Public Safety During the Terror,* Princeton: Princeton University Press, 1941.

Plamenatz, John, *The Revolutionary Movement in France, 1815-1871,* London: Longmans, 1952.

Ruggiero, Guido de, *The History of European Liberalism,* tr. by R. G. Collingwood, London: Oxford University Press, 1927.

Schapiro, J. Salwyn, *Liberalism and the Challenge of Fascism,* New York: McGraw-Hill, 1949.

Scott, John A., *Republican Ideas and the Liberal Tradition in France, 1870-1914,* New York: Columbia University Press, 1951.

Soltau, Roger, *French Political Thought in the Nineteenth Century,* New Haven: Yale University Press, 1931.

Wolf, J. B., *France, 1815 to the Present,* New York: Prentice-Hall, 1940.

INDEX

VAN NOSTRAND ANVIL BOOKS already published